New Directions for a Musical Church

# *New Directions*
# *for a Musical Church*

by PETER STAPLETON

**JOHN KNOX PRESS**
ATLANTA

Chapter 2, by the author, was previously published in article form as
"Coping with the Recruitment Myth." Reprinted by permission from
JOURNAL OF CHURCH MUSIC, vol. 16, no. 8, September 1974.
Copyright, Fortress Press.

The "Leadership Self-Assessment Checklist" found in the Appendix is
adapted by the author from "Leadership Self-Assessment Instrument,"
The Network of Innovative Schools, Merrimac, Massachusetts, and is
used with permission.

**Library of Congress Cataloging in Publication Data**

Stapleton, Peter, 1943—
    New directions for a musical church.

    1. Church music.   2. Choirs (Music)   I. Title.
MT88.S824N5        783.8        75-13452
ISBN 0-8042-1765-3

© John Knox Press 1975
Printed in the United States of America

# ACKNOWLEDGEMENTS

I owe special debts of gratitude to those whose care, skill, and achievement continue to inspire work in the music of the church:

Most particularly to Claude Means, first teacher, kind friend, and lasting influence;

To clergy: The Right Rev. Robert B. Appleyard; The Rev. E. Walter Chater; The Rev. Richard E. Gary;

To choirs: All Saints' Church, Harrison, New York; Saint Mary's, Manhattanville, New York City; The Church of the Messiah, Auburndale, Massachusetts, where most of the experiences in this book occurred;

To ladies: My mother, Janice Firth, who even went so far as to sing soprano under my direction; and to Faith Howland Kaiser, whose aid and support far exceed deserving.

P.T.S.
Provincetown, Massachusetts
August, 1974

# CONTENTS

# INTRODUCTION

How Shall We Sing the Lord's Song in a Foreign Land?

As the twentieth century rolls into its last quarter, a major new affliction affects us. It is what Alvin Toffler has called Future Shock—the staggering realization that tomorrow is here today, that the past is gone before it's even been the present, that we must suddenly and quickly cope with a world we do not really recognize or understand.

Technology has increased the rate of change in societies with such force that mere human beings are often at a loss to make sense of the new world around them.

If accelerated change is a problem for modern professionals—managers, scientists, technocrats themselves—it is even more of a problem for those who serve the church. Clergy, generalists by trade, are confronted with a society of specialists. Musicians, trained as specialists, are confronted with the very threat of obsolescence.

Perhaps most bewildering is feeling that we do not know who is in control of the changes taking place around us. Big business bows to technology, technology looks to government for subsidies, and government, it seems, can barely keep track of its operations, much less perform them effectively. A sense of anarchy and futility creeps upon us periodically which constitutes a new and frightening professional challenge.

The challenge is: Can we cope with inevitable ambiguity in our work and particularly in our role as church musicians? For much of society the role of church musicians is not only ambiguous, it is unheard-of! To clarify who we are and what we do, we may have to ask some essential questions of definition.

## What Is Church Music?

Are we a musical church? Can we be? Do we wish to be a musical church in the light of so many changes and urgent demands in a crisis-filled world? What role does music have in the church anyway?

Not every church which now makes music is a professionally musical church. An enormous amount of what we hear in churches is a kind of folk music. It may be written by Bach or Faure, or even Ned Rorem or Richard Felciano. But the performances are unmistakably folksy: beauty created as often by accident, by good intentions, or by chance as by design or training. Church music is usually practiced by amateurs, often volunteers. The fact that many of us have professional ambitions does not change our amateur status.

Nor is amateurism bad. There is clearly a place for folk artists in the church. They are authentic, involving, human, and concerned to give aesthetic expression to deep human and theological truth.

This state of affairs does not inevitably make fine art, however. Despite attempts to be "professional," few of us are fine artists. We are folk artists doing a fine job. Not all churches believe that we must all try harder to make our choirs and instruments sound like the concert hall. The church's dilemma is to examine how it may best sound like the church. Concert-like results are called for only in some particular settings. In too many churches, the attempt to give concerts fails sadly. When this failure continues, it looks first pretentious, then silly, then pathetic, and finally painful in its death agonies. If church music is a fluidly defined folk art, what is the definition of its practitioners?

## Who Is the Church Musician?

For the last two hundred years, the church musician has been the poor relation of the concert artist. Because the American frontier culture has often demanded a variety of skills for survival, the church musician has often had non-musical roles to play— teacher, professional, barber, carpenter. Most of the exceptions prove the rule.

American church music has a rich and varied history, but it is not the history of uninterrupted professionalism yielding the flowers of centuries of cultivation. It is a history similar to the development of other branches of U. S. culture: pragmatic, inventive, rough-and-ready. True to cultural tradition, then, the church musician's identity today will probably be formulated in a typically American way by ingenious synthesizers; by inventors rather than by traditionalists or scholars. Church music skills often develop on the job rather than in formal training. Our work will probably be more pragmatic than scholarly.

Many church musicians are creating a role for themselves in each situation they encounter. Few act out a clearly defined role which can be universally effective. Already 'new titles spring up like Minister to the Jazz Community, or Director of Fine Arts. These titles imply kinds of expertise more varied—maybe more comprehensive—than in the past.

Guitar-playing, cocktail piano improvisation, the literature and materials of Rock—are these the new requisites in the church musician's repertoire? Instead of Sacred Music Specialists are we simply Secular Music Generalists? Will the church ask musicians for skills no different from what the dance hall asks for?

It could be. If "secular" theology establishes that the traditional understanding of God is expendable, can Bach stay sacred? Maybe concert halls will be far more receptive to our traditional skills and repertoire than churches. But for many churches God is not dead yet. New challenges simply mean new patterns of meaning and worship will emerge. For some churches, musicians may be called to reaffirm the worth of fine music written for the church, for the choir, the organ.

## The New Role

Out of the underlying realities of our work comes one new identity for the church musician. The church musician is now a change agent: for the church, for music, for himself. Change, the new permanence, will affect us all. We have the choice between being its passive victims or its active agents. Being change agents does not mean that we must always be radical innovators. We may simply help transitions to work smoothly and rationally, sometimes even slowly. One important task may be to purvey the traditional musical virtues of finely executed organ playing and artistic choral direction. Another task may be to goad or intrigue or motivate.

Social Scientist Ronald Havelock describes a change agent as a combination of three people: a catalyst, a process helper, a solution giver. Musicians have performed these functions in churches for a long time. We have been catalysts by introducing new music, by motivating people to appreciate or make better music. We have been process helpers by teaching, preparing performances, planning services, or developing programs. We have been solution givers in solving musical problems and providing specialized skills and insights to the church's life. Today we may recognize our change agent roles more clearly than before. Many of the change agent's functions we perform with great skill already. We can develop them, use them more consciously and more often.

What will reward these new efforts? First, ways may emerge for musicians who now worry about their future to serve invaluably in the development of church life. The healing functions of beauty, the spiritual and moral power of live music are needed more than ever. The contributions of musical art can continue to enrich human life, so that a ministry in music may be one of the church's most powerful forms of witness.

Second, music itself, not just the church, can benefit. The human dimensions of study, rehearsal, and performance may be enhanced in both old and new forms of music in church. As a humanistic pursuit, music is spread through the devotion of its artists and composers addressing the world around them. This endeavor is too precious to lose in a flurry of secularization and technological advance.

This book seeks to expand the boundaries of church music practice by reaching out to new methodologies, helping musicians in churches to preserve and build upon a rich tradition.

# PART ONE: Gearing Up

These three chapters describe strategies for a look at what music can do.

Working in groups is an effective way to approach initial steps of musical development. Groups don't need to be experts to be effective. Anyone interested in music may be qualified to help with gathering opinions, setting goals, recruiting talent.

How?

Using simple formats for informal meetings, the groups described here helped to begin some crucial activities. Instead of passing the buck to the organist, people helped him focus on what was needed. By reviewing together and planning together, church people can give music the support and involvement it needs to succeed.

# 1

## SETTING GOALS: WHERE DO WE GO FROM HERE?

Diversity of motivations and personnel is often a problem in focusing the efforts of choral groups. The following experience with a Junior College Glee Club, the Orphean Society, was no exception. For a church dealing with an increasing diversity in its population instead of the more homogenous congregation of earlier times, this experience may be helpful.

Students in the group showed some interest in singing, but it was hard to know how it could be nurtured. The administration recognized some students who wanted to sing, and gave the Society an allowance for the director's part-time salary, as in a church program. Beyond those two gestures, though, the group's direction was unclear.

What happened to (1) sharpen the goals of the undertaking, and (2) meet as many expectations as possible? Initially, students responded well to an invitation to "join Orphean." Although they were not sure what to expect, almost fifty students appeared for the first meeting. Far in excess of expectations, the turnout showed potential for a musical undertaking. After several rehearsals, however, it was clear that the group needed more sense of what it was about. The youths seemed to enjoy the music, but attendance was not consistent. No one seemed sure to what this program was leading or whether or not it deserved time in a busy undergraduate schedule.

As director, I faced the perennial teacher's dilemma: impose a direction and risk loss of students' enthusiasm, or cater to a vaguely low expectation, and risk a vapid experience for himself and the singers.

We needed guidelines to help make the group viable. To derive guidelines, I assumed that:

> Students should participate to the maximum extent in defining their group,
>
> Administration and faculty should have a voice in defining how the group should proceed,
>
> The director's role should be to help students and administration and faculty reach *their* goals rather than setting up his own goals.

Orphean was not a very clear concept to most people on campus. As a result we were free to set up any guidelines we wished. Where traditional expectations define what a group and what its director should do, such flexibility might not be possible. Here we had freedom to create whatever musical organization might evolve.

At an early rehearsal the Orphean Society singers received no music to sing. Instead, each singer was asked to write down a one-sentence answer to the questions:

> What should Orphean accomplish?
>
> What are its reasons for existing?

The questions were designed to provoke answers giving students' *reasons* to sing with Orphean rather than activities which only gave students Things To Do.

After each singer had completed the list, small groups of six formed to share their lists. Sextets then listed together, in order of priority, what goals the group felt were most important.

After thirty minutes of thinking, listening, discussing, and prioritizing, small groups reported ten shared reasons for the existence of their glee club:

> To teach singing
>
> To be taken seriously as a musical activity

To give concerts of choral music in conjunction with male
glee clubs
To stage informal music for college functions
To sing varied kinds of music
To create informal social occasions
To sing for hospitals or shut-in groups
To encourage singers to suggest repertoire
To get members together socially
To give enjoyment

It wasn't easy to put these in order of priority. "We ought to do
all of them," people said. But limitations of time, energy, and
resources would require the group to find some cardinal goals to
guide it. After twenty minutes the group agreed on the following
three goals in order of importance:

To give enjoyment
To teach singing
To perform

Of course, these are obvious reasons for a glee club to exist.
Articulating them this way, though, allowed several desirable
conclusions:

1) Students told me that enjoyment was the primary objective
—so repertoire and rehearsal styles should be tailored to that objective first.

2) Students had spelled out for each other that Orphean was a
learning activity and should provide learning opportunities. This
meant that a teaching director would be responding to his singers'
desires rather than appearing to legislate his own wishes. Learning by request rather than by fiat was particularly vital to the
morale of a strictly volunteer group.

3) Students recognized that their meetings should have some
musical purpose rather than "just doing it for the fun of it" as the
first goal might suggest, or "just doing it to learn" as the second
goal might indicate.

4) Students realized that to attain their goals some follow-up on
the session would be needed. A task force of eight students agreed
to meet after rehearsal to plan strategies with me.

5) Students achieved a feeling of "owning" shared goals.

The task force identified several next steps: arranging a caroling expedition at Christmas, writing letters to other college singing groups to promote an exchange concert, even investigating a trip to the Caribbean during spring vacation.

Meanwhile questionnaires for key administrators and faculty—asking the same questions students had addressed—provided additional input. Interestingly, they supported the very objectives set down by students.

The head of the Music Department, deans, and even the president contributed to the group by writing their ideas on goals, activities, and next steps.

Perhaps singers cannot achieve every goal they hope for. Perhaps a goal-setting session should begin every new year. In any case, the exercise paid off in a feeling of momentum and interest students sensed and reported. They felt the chorus was becoming a going concern with some directions in which to move.

By giving students and colleagues a share in setting those directions, the director learns what expectations already lie within the group itself. If the people involved feel that they are meeting their needs and providing the kind of musical activity which they want, this experiment may help encourage enthusiastic participation in choral singing.

# 2

## COPING WITH THE RECRUITMENT MYTH

"Getting bigger and bigger is getting better and better," goes a particular myth of American progress.

"Expand the program" is a less grand but related charge faced in many forms, sometimes unspoken, by music directors, clergy, or committees.

There are few countervailing influences—perhaps the commercial success of Volkswagens is an exception—to urge smallness. Even the determined speeches of some theologians who say "quality is more important than quantity; getting small may be good; what an opportunity for Christian growth," or the like, often have the ring of rationalization. Although social critics tell us that the Vietnam War taught the dangers of expanding operations to be effective, the urge for bigness is still an American instinct.

What does this have to do with church music? Simply this: The desire for bigness in the next ten years may be a serious hindrance to qualitative progress in our churches. When records and media can make big noises and play the strains of large and superb choirs to the people we serve, few of those people can fail to make unfavorable comparisons with what they hear in church.

This is not to say that members should not be added to the musical enterprise of the parish, or that it is foolish to include as many people as possible in a musical experience at church. But the desire to expand for expansion's sake is fraught with peril.

Problems arise unless that desire is supported by goals clear to people involved and deliberate strategies for achieving such goals.

It is the purpose of this chapter (1) to show that direct unexamined recruitment in behalf of any church group—in this case the choir—can be ineffectual and even harmful, and (2) to point out three alternative means of group action which can aid self-renewal, without a "recruitment program."

## I. The Source of Group Power

George Peabody, the psychologist and educator, posits the following: Groups derive power from sharing common goals which they understand and believe to be valid.

In a time of fragmentation and disunity, many groups find it difficult to share, explore, and support common goals. Disunity in political parties, for instance, can indicate that goals to which a majority once subscribed can fragment into goals not shared by a large group.

If Peabody's theory is correct that shared goals—not group size—create power, choir singers' goals are important to share in the group (and with the director!). It may be necessary to spend some considerable time on goal-setting to achieve a consensus on what goals the group shares and considers valid. If the time and concern now expended on recruitment were expended on defining goals first, perhaps the progress of a church group could proceed more effectively.

## II. Goals and Activities: Why the Difference Can Be Crucial

Committees hiring musicians are sometimes honest enough to state that one of their prime concerns is "to have more people in the choir." Usually one person adds, "the way we used to."

These people would like good music too, mind you. Both quality and quantity are important. But, to be truthful, they want "more" bodies in the choir loft. Their goal? More people. The activity to reach the goal? Good music. How could there be any doubt that these two elements are incompatible?

It is bewildering for such a committee to hear the flaws in their reasoning. A steady diet of what most organists consider "good" music may be one of the least effective strategies for meeting the goal of "bigness."

Some groups may be mistaking their activities for their goals ("We always have a card party in October"; "Isabel has sung that solo every Good Friday for the last twenty years" are comments which might indicate that confusion between goals and activities is present).

Sometimes activities linger on whose goals are unclear. When worship activities, for instance, fail to address human goals—e.g. to comfort, to pray, to sing, to learn—they often fail to engage meaningful participation. Musical activities need to relate directly to shared goals.

### III. The Counterproductive Effect of Recruitment

Americans may be a nation of joiners by reputation, but they seem warier today than they have been. One example of such public caution is found in the increasing difficulty of leaders in engaging followers. Perhaps this is a healthy sign in our culture. It does not help the choir director who is charged with recruiting potential singers.

Invitations which look like they are rendered "from the top down" can hurt a program more than helping. Even if singers accept such an invitation, it may be out of a sense of duty, or pity, or sheer inability to say no. The "duty" people soon find themselves chafing at their role. The "pity" ones are seldom motivated to take initiative. The "inability" people may derive comfort from their experience, but may not grow in the experience as church leaders would wish.

Usually, a member of the group is a more effective recruiter than the leader. Ideally, everyone in the enterprise invites participation. A feeling of "Come sing with us" is more inviting than a suggestion of "Come sing for me." While any single person with a monopoly on recruitment activity can inhibit initiative from others, this is especially true when the sole recruiter is the leader—either by his choice or the group's insistence. If a group is not motivated to share the validity and clarity of its goals with others, it is in trouble. Seeking new members is a group process to be shared.

## IV. Three Steps Toward Renewal

Setting goals
Matching goals and activities
Recruiting by group members

These three processes may not be easy at first. Firstly, few people consider the reasons behind their accustomed behavior. A choir motivated by habit or nostalgia may voice concern that goals should even need to be shared. Once engaged in looking at goals, they may be surprised to see the diversity of reasons people have for being in the choir. By the same token, they may be encouraged to see how many goals they share in common. By sharing goals, they can develop a stronger sense of being a united team with consciously stated reasons for being together, rather than a "fuzzy" club ruled vaguely by good intentions. Secondly, activities to meet goals effectively may be different from the activities now going on. A choir whose goal is to lead the hymn-singing may not find the activity of rehearsing anthems relevant to its mission.

A choir explicitly responsible for leading hymns may draw a larger number of singers than a choir aimed at singing challenging choral repertoire. In one church, having "high quality" choral music meant *reducing* the number of singers and changing rehearsal patterns for part of the year. The change paid off when singers joined a small group with clear goals. When it was a larger group, uncertain in focus, members had failed to join. A good "fit" between goals and activities is one way to encourage singers to support their group. People can feel they share goals and support appropriate activities.

Thirdly, choir members may find roles of responsibility new to them. A renewal effort through goal-setting and choosing activities may bring unexpected challenges. New skills of diplomacy and new ways of thinking about what the choir is may both have to be introduced to parish singers.

If the challenge is real, the payoffs are just as real. The clarification involved in defining a group can be invaluable. Ideally, it can build teamwork, define areas of responsibility, and align activities with values and goals of members.

## Conclusion

Recruitment is not a musical goal. It is not a musical activity. Recruitment needs to be set in perspective as it relates to the church's goals and activities. If a group can begin to acquire the three skills of self-renewal described in this chapter, it can cope with the recruitment myth. Perhaps the group may even replace the myth with a rational process leading to a successful evolution for musicians in groups.

# 3

## CHURCH MUSIC CHECKUP: A DESIGN FOR REVIEWING THE PARISH PROGRAM

How do participants in a parish music program feel about it? Apathetic? Enthusiastic? Does the choir have the same view as the congregation about how they sound? How about the clergy?

Where can a musician find answers for these questions?

This design for a group meeting is one way to collect data about a music program's basic health. The results in the case shown here showed strengths as well as concerns, and allowed the participants to take next steps toward improvement.

Several objectives are met when the design is used. The benefits include:

> Building awareness of the program,
> Involving parishioners in an honest review of what's working and what isn't,
> Fostering interest and commitment toward making any needed changes.

Several changes of procedure in the music program had taken place when this meeting was called. The parish was grappling with many changes in its worship life, and had a new minister as well. It was important in this review of the music for people to feel free to discuss their feelings about the changes. It was also important that the congregation (as well as the "pros" in the choir) be invited to share the review.

The desired outcome was a feeling that more people could be involved in music than just the choir, and that these people—congregation and choir—could affect the course of events. We wanted to overcome the sense that the minister and organist made all the decisions (and did most of the work!).

Of course, as Director of Music, I had set goals when making changes. My question was: Are the goals being met? Do we really have more variety, higher quality, and greater integrity in our music than we have had? Here is how I asked the parish for the answers.

The choir agreed to a meeting for review of the program. Next, the parish at large was invited in announcements in church and in writing, giving everyone at least three weeks notice. The choir has had periodic informal talks about their work before. This was the first time that others had been invited to join.

Once assembled, the group was given paper, pencils, and instructions. Each person was asked to list three strengths and three concerns about the music since September. The frame of reference was clearly set in the recent past; I was not desirous of hearing where that nice alto had moved who sang for Easter three years ago, or about what a fine baritone the last rector had, or what a shame that we didn't have the anthems we used to. The point was to find out what people thought of things happening now!

After the lists were written, the group broke into pairs. The task for each pair was to achieve agreement on three strengths and three concerns they could say they shared. This invited discussion or argument which would involve everyone without giving a few strong voices the power to dominate the meeting.

With their set of strengths and concerns, the pairs were asked to join larger groups. Once again they would share their ideas. The task was to listen to the lists, and then reach agreement on three strengths and three concerns shared by that group. The results of group work were then reported to the entire meeting. In this way everyone could see what was considered strong about our music, as well as what we needed to know to improve.

I recorded the strengths and concerns on newsprint pads to make them more graphic for the group. Results were:

Strengths:  Music program has variety
Quality is high
People support the program

Because these strengths were so close to the goals of the program, they were exciting to see emerging from the large group.

Concerns:  Choir attendance is spotty
Services sometimes need more planning
Rehearsal times are too short

With these concerns very much on the music director's mind, it was helpful—even comforting—to see that others shared them too. It was also helpful to many people to see that others shared their perceptions. Sharing is important in a church where many issues of change and policy may be points of controversy. In music we were helping to absorb a major change for what it was worth—evaluating, instead of arguing, as we went.

As a final step in the forty minutes, I used five minutes to see if the meeting had effectively involved the participants. The three questions asked to gauge this were:

Was the meeting helpful in clarifying what we're trying to do?
Was it interesting to you?
Would you come to another meeting like this?

Everyone recorded his answer on a scale of 1 to 10 (1 meaning an enthusiastic "yes," 10, a hearty "no."). Happily enough, there were a large number responding affirmatively, indicating that the discussion format had won approval, and that people would even come back for more.

But now what? After reviewing your program, are there next steps to take toward effective improvement? The obvious reply is: Build on the strengths and address the concerns. For example, I now know that variety, rather than the same two-page-anthem form of musical activity, is appreciated by those at the meeting as well as by me. This information gives me a mandate to continue programming a wide assortment of offerings. I will be able to do this knowing that the goal I envisioned—to have more varied kinds of music—is a goal people share. I won't be too far out on a limb in their eyes or mine. This kind of comfort and support is important to the practitioner of any art as volatile and challenging as church music.

In addressing concerns I will begin to call on people who attended the meeting. For instance, since we are now agreed that rehearsal attendance is spotty, there may be those concerned enough to organize themselves to solve the problem by making phone calls or sending letters.

The involvement from this meeting will have at least two payoffs. First, rehearsal attendance may improve if the group finds an effective strategy. Second, a group from this meeting will be addressing the problem together rather than a harried music director struggling with the problem alone. Since people have indicated willingness to attend another meeting, at least we have made a start.

This exercise can also be a check on the director. If the group's ideas are far removed from what the director thinks are strengths and concerns of the music program, some adjustments may be needed. Either the director needs to check his goals to see if they are clear and realistic, or he may need a way to communicate more effectively with the people he serves. A meeting like this can be a start in setting or assessing goals together.

Collecting feedback, setting goals, coping with the prospect of change: all these are activities to help move a music program forward. By using this simple design, or a version of it which works for you, a parish can begin—at virtually any point in the course of its program—a form of evaluation for heading toward success.

# PART TWO: Progress Step by Step

Even in trying to stay the same, many churches face the prospect of change. But is change progress?

Mastering old skills like music-reading may be as important as learning new ones, like selecting the right folk song from innumerable options.

People, materials, program—how do they best fit together? Each church looks for the combination suited to its particular character.

These chapters describe processes for finding what can work best. Step by step, the experience of deliberate development can provide for human growth as well as musical excitement.

# 4

## HERE COMES THE RESOURCE EXPLOSION!

The vast amount of music and materials available to churches today staggers the imagination. Publishers bombard us with new offerings all too convincingly packaged. Journals review new editions and publications monthly. The music stores burst with new trends. Even the grapevine of clergy and singers yields new discoveries designed to spur our flock into new fealty to the gospel.

### Stop the Music

With this constant flow of material, there must be a process to sort out relevant resources and place them where they can be most effective. The steps in this chapter cannot determine what music will or will not serve a particular church. They can help a committee or musician to go about finding those materials a church truly will and can use.

There is simply too much material to choose from if churches simply browse through what they are offered. We need to change this pattern. Churches need to become the active seekers of the right materials for their particular needs, rather than the passive recipients of publishers or even libraries.

We need to know what we are looking for. But how can we know what we mean until we've heard what we've said? And once we specify some "perfect item," how can we be sure that it exists—our hoped-for treasure?

Here's a way to begin.

## STEP 1—Clarifying

What needs does the church program have? A new Easter anthem? A collection of easy pieces for three-part chorus? A method for introducing rhythm instruments to the youth group?

If a church can begin to identify its needs even this specifically, the first steps in beating the resource explosion is well under way. The following process of clarification involves:

> Identifying needs or areas of interest,
> Assessing them, talking and thinking them through,
> Defining as clearly as possible what materials will meet the needs identified.

The clarification process, like many designs in this book, is most creatively used in groups. The advantages of looking for material in a group include:

> Greater variety of suggestions,
> Sharing of musical viewpoints,
> Possibility for creative compromise,
> "Ownership" of the new materials, a shared responsibility for them which will aid their acceptance once they are used.

The musician may still be the final decision-maker. The group he works with, though, will have a better insight into his decision if they share it, at least in the beginning.

To help clarify what materials are needed, the musician should have a format in mind for how the group will guide its discussions. One discussion format might aim to answer the following questions:

Who will use this material? Congregation, senior choir, youth, perhaps several groups?

When will this material be introduced?

What should this material accomplish in the program? Provide an experience with jazz liturgy, expand repertoire of the Baroque era in the senior choir, reinforce a particular theme?

What restrictions need to be observed? Length, difficulty, available instruments, stylistic considerations?

What sources would be most likely to provide the needed materials? Catalogues of works by a popular composer, particular
collections, instruction books?

How can we best describe what material we're looking for? (Such
as "an anthem for unison voices with two recorders in a folk
idiom for Mother's Day.")

How will we look for such materials?

Who will help the search and how?

Negotiating needs for materials lets people involved with the
church's music share some interests about what directions they
see in the program and where it might be heading. A church need
not even have a choir to engage in a negotiating session.

Sharing perspectives and views challenges fixed opinions. Those
who contribute "We need to get back to the good old hymns" will
have to answer convincingly the voices of those who want more
guitars in the sanctuary. The session may become a chance to
channel musical controversy into some creative compromise
which unites people in addressing needs. The voiced desires of
individuals can sometimes become the shared goals of group action. At the very least negotiating allows people to be heard.

With the clearly voiced results of a negotiation group churches
may begin to avoid the sad try-and-fail-again method of plough-
ing through materials which "just might work." Careful negotiation aims to avoid the fatiguing and discouraging results of guess-
work.

Far from being a kind of structured bull session in which most
contributions begin "Why don't we try . . . ," the negotiation is
directed at articulating a group's expression of its need. Participants can feel that they can affect the choice of their church's
music, and that they share a task together in finding that music.
They do not have to wait in hope that the hapless musician will
make a lucky guess about an anthem, nor fear his making a sad
mistake about a new hymn.

Looking at needs and their possible answers, some member of
the group—the musician, or a minister with skills in human relations, or the chairman of the music committee—may take an
important helping role in the session. The helping person may

check the group's progress by looking for specific kinds of behavior.

Questions like the following can help a group seeking to be specific in clarifying needs for musical material:

1. Is the group defining only one need, or several separate needs which will require several separate kinds of material?

2. Is the musician involved listening and understanding the kinds of needs under discussion?

3. Is someone able to record in writing what the group is specifying as its needs? A recorder may read back what he hears in a negotiation to be sure the group is clear about what it has said.

4. Are group members sharing accurately and specifically what materials seem to be needed? Kinds of materials (if not specific works) should be specified as clearly as possible. This way, with mounting costs, expenditure for materials can be responsibly accounted for. Donors may even be found to support a particular project who would not contribute simply "to buy more music."

5. Does the group need training or practice, or simply more time in stating its feelings about needed material?

6. If experimental material—jazz or rock—is being considered, is its use being clearly defined? Some such music may be for a one-shot single occasion, and could be borrowed or rented.

7. Does everyone understand who will make the decisions about materials? People need reassurance about who will use their ideas (committee, organist, minister, or a combination of these) and how.

8. Are group members sharing opinions about particular materials or simply about generalized preferences? Both are valuable, but they need to be recognized for what they are.

9. Has the group agreed on a written description of needed materials by the end of the session?

10. Is it clear how the search for the needed materials will proceed? Who will help and how?

At first, a clarification session may be full of ambiguities and perhaps some confusion. This is natural. People will have many thoughts to express about music they know or wish to know. All of these thoughts should be used to point to the work of the session.

The leader needs to be aware that there will probably be more ideas than fewer. He will be responsible to bring the group gently back to the task of specific statements when it wanders or becomes confused with the amount and variety of input from its members.

A simple restatement of the task may help: "Our task here is simply to be as specific as we can about materials we'll need to implement our music program." The recorder of the group's thinking will be responsible for writing and then restating for the group a clear expression of what materials will be sought.

A group may wish to search for several different kinds of material. If the group generates a number of needs, the leader may have to ask for some ordering of priorities, so that the search and acquisition process may be orderly and reasoned. Few can afford the "big splurge" which costs money and may not be addressed to specific needs in the church's future.

STEP 2—Retrieving

Once the clarifying group has written a description of needed materials they ask: Where do we look now? Who will provide us with what we need?

Most musicians have a favorite answer for these questions. We like to browse through a favorite store, or make a special trip to the city for the hunt. Or we reach for the newest catalogue from that publisher where we have a charge account.

Actually, like the numerous materials available, there are numerous sources. The purpose of this step is to look at a wide range of musical sources in order to plan an effective search for the needed materials.

There is such an array of riches in the varying sources that no church need merely settle for what is close at hand. What's more, new means are constantly being devised for the dissemination of first-rate resources available to all kinds of situations.

When librarians identify sources of information, they sometimes refer to what is called a bibliographic chain. A bibliographic chain refers to the sequence in which information passes through time. New scientific information, for instance, begins in the head of a scientist, then moves to a journal, then to an index, then a bibliography, then an encyclopedia. Scientist—Journal—Index—Bibliography—Encyclopedia. As the information becomes more mature, it moves into a wider range of well-documented sources.

Musical materials like the Bach cantatas and other mature and well-established works may be found in many sources (libraries, various publishers editions, journals reporting musicological insights for their history and interpretation). They are well established in many links of the bibliographic chain. A new avant-garde work—such as a Rod McKuen text set for bicycle pump and electronic tape—may still be in manuscript at a local university. This kind of material will be found in a different part of the bibliographic chain because it is new and still awaiting wider dissemination.

By looking at many links in the bibliographic chain, a church may be able to have access to many new or "obscure" materials perfect for its use, which simply are not readily available to the wide audience as are more conventional or familiar music.

Here are six links in a bibliographic chain devised for finding church music materials:

Human Resources
Institutional Resources
Journals
Books
Bibliographies
Commercial Resources

Human Resources:

In the age of computer data banks, human word-of-mouth information is still of vital importance. Talk still tells a story unavailable in other ways. For example: "Sure we tried it because it looked easy and I heard it at a workshop, but our sopranos couldn't get the intervals without an extra rehearsal, and the people didn't like the words. Thought they were too obscure and didn't relate to the church." Candor can seldom be as effective in print, and it seldom comes from music sellers.

Colleagues, teachers, even chance acquaintances at workshops may yield important insight about what will be effective. Consulting a composer could yield information, or, if the composer doesn't know a piece for rhythm band, piano and bass, he might write one! Friendly neighbors may even lend music which fits the description of what a church is seeking.

Institutional Resources:

Organizations abound to aid the musical church. Denominations maintain bodies such as the Joint Office of Worship of the PCUS and UPCUSA, the Presbyterian Association of Musicians, the Unitarian Religious Arts Guild, the Lutheran Commission on Worship and the Arts, and the Episcopal Joint Commission on Church Music. These groups compile lists and circulate bibliographies of music for particular occasions or for particular resources.

In this ecumenical age, information may easily be exchanged across denominational lines. Roman Catholic bodies such as the National Catholic Music Educators' Association and Jewish councils on Sacred Music have much to share with churches interested in a wide range of choice. Musical organizations include the American Guild of Organists with its increasingly active Committee on Sharing Resources, the Choristers' Guild, and the National Association of Teachers of Singing. In addition, many university music schools have departments of church music able to make recommendations and suggestions.

In using institutional resources, a church seeking a single anthem or an instructional method may discover an irresistable cantata or jazz liturgy. These happy and useful surprises can be encouraged. Often they occur when more than one person becomes involved in the search for materials.

Journals:

In addition to the American Guild of Organists' *Music,* there are denominational monthlies such as the Roman Catholic *Sacred Music,* Lutheran *Journal of Church Music,* Methodist *Music Ministry,* and *Reformed Liturgy and Music* of the Presbyterian Church, U. S. Music educators' periodicals may help. A reference librarian may help compile a list of those journals in print which review new materials regularly. Often such magazines report performances of particular works, and the study of a review may be helpful to a church which wants to find out what a performance of chancel opera or a multi-media presentation involves.

Books:

In the bibliographic chain, books on music do not usually provide the most recent information. But they are too obvious to overlook. Church music volumes contain bibliographies, discographies, and/or music lists depending on their particular slant. Choral music is thoroughly written about, mostly by music educators. Literature for the contemporary church is more difficult to locate. Many church musicians still repair to the classic *Protestant Church Music in America* written four decades ago by Archibald Davison, or Donald Kettring's *Steps Toward a Singing Church*, reflecting the movement into graded choir programs during the prosperous fifties. Lists of books belong to another part of the bibliographic chain.

Bibliographies:

Lists aren't always exciting, but they're indispensable aids to a comprehensive search, especially in the beginning stages. A church will certainly want a collection of secondary sources in order to plan the widest range of alternative choices. The catalogues of neighboring churches can be helpful to exchange or borrow music. A search or familiarity with the catalogue of university music libraries may provide scholarly help enriching a church's options.

Commercial Resources:

Many churches feel at the mercy of salesmen. The resources of stores aren't the best place to start, but of course they're useful. Browsing for fun and profit is too dear an activity to most of us to be discounted. The warning: be sure you have your ideas from the clarifying session well in hand. That way, you can avoid the feeling of "being had" by salespeople who can't really understand your particular needs. Publishers, of course, (even ones in

England, Germany, Austria) will happily send catalogues and often samples of their wares directly to you.

## Where to Begin?

Look for key words describing what your clarifying groups saw as needs: "anthems," "easy," "youth choir," "familiar arrangements." Do they suggest that one resource area may be more likely than others?

Alternatively, pick one area you feel will most likely yield good results. What are the reasons for your choice? As you review why you chose a particular resource area you will sharpen skills in finding resources.

Knowing the various resource areas and how to enter them—always with negotiation results in hand—will help make you more adept at emerging from the jungle of resources with the trophies you need in hand.

As the search continues it may be helpful to keep a record of who was consulted, what areas were explored, and what materials were considered if not chosen. This information may aid later searches, could be helpful to other churches, or might even be publishable in a church magazine or musical journal. Such a record need not be elaborate. A format such as the following may help clarify the process:

Statement of Need:
Resources Consulted:
Results Acquired:
Final Choice:
Observations:

## STEP 3—Communicating

With so many resources available, even a well-organized searcher may find himself overloaded with materials which come close to what is sought. What happens, then, if he finds something which doesn't fit the description? What is the fate of a choir director who began to look for an Easter anthem and discovered a program of handbells, or a Lenten sequence of motets for women's chorus?

Obviously, finding materials is a task so varied and rich that it will open endless doors and possibilities. If materials beckon which are not specified in the description, simply renegotiate. This is advisable on several counts: First, if the search doesn't yield what a group expects, there may be hurt feelings or misunderstanding. "We wanted a cantata, not a jam session," says one soprano. How well can the eager musician explain a jazz cantata? If she is consulted before materials are acquired, life may be smoother. Second, as a group becomes more aware of what resources are available, it may develop more alternative interests. As interest and sophistication grow, the group or the musician sees ways of making richer options than were present.

Why settle for another anthem, if a search reveals a good collection? Why stop at a cantata if an oratorio fits what people would enjoy working on? A musician or a group need never be afraid to renegotiate their needs or interests. This may involve looking at what a preliminary search has found, or hearing reports from one or two searchers who feel they have hit pay-dirt of a particular kind.

### STEP 4—Evaluating the Process

We have all heard the cry from congregations that "We never sing the Good Old Hymns anymore," which indicates that the relationship between people and materials ("All Those New Hymns") may not be ideal. Plain-song just doesn't turn them on like "Holy, Holy, Holy." Whatever people come to church expecting is not what they are finding and the result can be dissonance: between assumptions and activities, expectations and experience, sometimes between individuals or groups.

How can evaluation help?

First, if the search process is to yield music which will become part of the people's experience, we need to know what that experience is. Then we can see how effectively the search and the materials are working.

A sample format to gauge the effect of a new piece or set of materials might look like this:

Name of material:

How selected:
How used and when:
Was the piece in accordance with negotiated needs?
How was it received by choir? Congregation?
What particular comments did it draw? (No comment may be a comment.)
Will it bear repeating? As a regular feature of the program?
Other observations?

## Conclusion

The process we have seen may seem like a lengthy rigamarole to pick a new anthem!

"The last organist picked such lovely pieces. We never went through all of this before!"

Surely this process—negotiation, identifying and then searching resource areas, selection and evaluation—is a deliberate set of activities. It may even be more than a church will wish to undertake. But the process is one direction which can yield results for a musical church where music and its performance in a church setting are valued. The development of a musical church was never simple or easy. Yet for those not endowed with trained talent or many resources, the process can create more likelihood of creative musical activity.

The materials to make music can be the crucial ingredients in church musical life. The tastes and associations and often the deepest meanings of a church's message are expressed in its music. Finding the most articulate and appropriate texts and settings can be a task of the greatest significance.

By following the steps of this chapter, the process of serious discussion and research can bring people together to share this important opportunity, even if they simply begin by exploring the parish music library together.

As new possibilities for performance emerge and the process of finding and acquiring the best new materials continues, a musical church will be encouraging new skills and a group of important resource people to aid its development.

# 5

## A MODULAR MUSIC PROGRAM

As you work to sustain a music program of quality in a small parish, try answering these simple questions: How many singers attend your choir rehearsal immediately after Christmas? After Easter? How successful is your tenor section? How excited are you about the music you can rehearse with the resources you have?

In the bleakest part of a New England winter, these questions passing through my mind had few inspiring answers about our parish. As some sociologists report, "too many too small" churches may have difficulty in either ending or resolving such questions.

Four central problems emerged.

1) Small Numbers: In a culture that likes things big, our church is small. The choir is smaller still and the last five years have seen it shrink from modest to "mini" proportions. Singers do not volunteer out of hand to sing for the church. The reasons for this may often be discussed. The fact remains that numerically, our resources are small.

2) Sameness: Often we are open to the criticism that one Sunday service is much like another. This can be a comforting strength in a historical tradition of worship. The effect on our singers, though, can be counter-productive. Either they chafe at the routineness of worship, or they move through comfortably but without real inspiration.

3) Goal-less-ness: Why *do* we keep our choirs operating? As a musician I am not used to spelling out why we have a choir for worship. Oh, it can be fun and a service to the parish, but more specifically it's often hard to say we're making fine music or adding substantive dimensions to people's lives.

4) Director-Dependency: The parish seemed to be looking to me to "provide the music." I felt alone in the responsibility for finding singers, finding music they could perform, and—most difficult—sustaining an inherited program which simply wasn't working.

I took these four problems to the choir at a rehearsal in March. We sat in a circle, sipped our coffee, and talked about them. At first, the predictable comments were made: Get more people, try harder, look at what other churches do. But we had tried to snare singers before, we were trying to make our system work, and other churches weren't doing much better than we were. What we needed was a plan different from our traditional every-Sunday four-part choir.

It was decided that we should look at a model which would address directly the problems we faced. The new program would:

Use small numbers effectively
Provide variety for singers and congregation
Meet specific musical goals
Involve singers in planning and implementation

Here is what we devised.

## A Modular Music Program

We divided the church season into six- or eight-week time periods. It was agreed that singers would only be asked to serve for these short time periods. This way an invitation to join the choir would not bind a singer into an indefinite commitment with indefinite purposes.

Singers agreed that in their social lives they would respond to a "Please come to dinner on Sunday" invitation more readily than to a "Drop in any time" invitation. Because a small choir must count on every one of its members to attend rehearsals and services, this short-duration plan aimed at asking every singer to be particularly faithful for a particular time.

By changing the content of rehearsals five times in the year—with a different kind of music in each period—we would address the problem of sameness. This did not mean that we would abandon altogether the four-part tradition we had enjoyed. It did mean that the traditional mode would be supplemented. We could also plan this change a year in advance, rather than plugging in novelties at random for the sake of novelty.

With a clear musical focus to each module the program would avoid the vague sing-along style of the not-so-hot choir. Because the church is near a major city, members are sensitive to the musical opportunities available nearby. By having clear musical goals, the program tries to offer musical integrity to singers who need to feel they are involved with an enterprise aiming for quality.

Each member of the choir received a copy of the plan for study. It was discussed at several meetings and modified by individuals. For instance, members seemed more interested in rehearsing early on Sundays than after a hard day's work on Thursdays. As the plan developed, singers even undertook to comb the music library for anthems suitable to particular modules. Involvement did not stop there. It became clear that invitations to the program would need to be issued four times per year rather than once. Increased contact with singers-at-large would require choir members to share in identifying and inviting would-be participants in the program.

Planning the Modules

When completed, the plan for the new program looked like Figure I. Although it could be different in a parish with different resources, we had particular reasons for designing our modular program this way. For instance, in our parish, we are fortunate to have a strong soprano section in the choir. Not unusually, we have more female singers than male ones. Therefore, since we wished to keep high quality, we began the year by focusing on developing the talent we had and learning new repertory suitable to that talent. We found that it doesn't hurt to start a new program with an element which is almost guaranteed of success!

## FIGURE I
## A Modular Music Program for 1972-1973

| Number of Weeks | Singers Needed | Rehearsal Focus | Service Music |
|---|---|---|---|
| 6 | Sopranos Altos | Treble repertoire, new music | 2, 3 part anthems, descants |
| 6 | Sopranos Altos Tenors Basses | 4 part anthems, Christmas music | 4 part hymns, chants, seasonal music |
| 8 | Varied | Small groups, solos, instruments | Congregational service music, solos, duets, folk mass |
| 6 | Sopranos Altos Tenors Basses | A cantata, familiar anthems, Lent and Easter music | Traditional choral music, specially prepared |
| 6 | Tenors Basses <br><br> or | Music for male voices | Anthems in TB arrangements, plainchant |
| | Volunteers in all parts | A joint choral project with other churches | Supplementary singers for hymns |

The four-part modules—which look much like our traditional program—have several advantages. First, they offer an experience which we have enjoyed and wish to preserve. Second, they culminate in major festivals—Christmas and Easter. This allows the choir to grow in numbers and enthusiasm as we prepare festival music without experiencing the "hangover" feeling of small numbers of singers after the holidays who take up their work again feeling let down.

During the winter, when post-Christmas lag may last too long, we have set time aside for an experimental module with a folk mass, solos, and a hymn sing. This succession of different offerings will lend interest to a season which needs spark. It also allows us to avoid the often-cited "keep 'em busy" tactic some of us must use to keep our choirs functional. In this module we also plan a mid-point review to ask choir and congregation how the music program is going, what it needs, how it might be improved. The absence of a choir-as-usual may spark some useful parish dialogue!

In the spring after Easter we have built in a choice of activities. We will see at that point if the men's chorus which the men suggested is still what singers want, or if other combinations have emerged from other modules.

### Advantages of the Program

As we use a modular scheme, the hoped-for advantages begin to emerge. We find:

> Singers respond to invitations when they are rendered at a particular time for a particular activity.
>
> Singers may enter the program together at the same time.
>
> More frequent contact with singers helps parish morale.
>
> A new format for recording contacts with potential musicians has been devised (see Figure II).
>
> We have given some dutiful male singers a much enjoyed chance to worship in the congregation for six weeks.
>
> The quality of choral sound has not diminished as had been feared.

We are still learning how best to use a modular music program.

As we learn, we seek to achieve musical integrity, to set goals, and to try new forms. For many of us this activity is as rewarding and productive as was the more traditional program, even when it was working smoothly. As a positive response to what critics often call negative conditions in the church, the modular program may be useful for our own enjoyment and as a strategy to share.

## FIGURE II

*Tally Sheet for Singers*

| Singer Called | By Whom | Date | Invitation Accepted | Invitation Deferred |
|---|---|---|---|---|
|  |  |  |  |  |

# 6

## REHEARSAL IN TRANSITION

### The Problem

What do you do? The choir has been away from rehearsals for two months. Christmas is a month away. How do you start preparing singers for a large task in a short time? Here are the hopes I had for the rehearsal to be explored in this chapter.

First, I wanted the group to move into its task by doing something active. Usually I present material, run through it, point out problems, and set about solving them. This time I wanted the singers themselves to consider the music seriously, and to develop some feeling for what had to be done. I wanted insights about the nature and dimension of the task to come from them.

Returning to a long rehearsal format after a long break, they would need a fresh experience. I wanted to avoid the "Here we go again," feeling which produces routine uninvolved participation. The rehearsal should be different somehow, with some new challenges and experiences to intrigue the group with what it was doing.

Questions as well as hopes arose. First, how well did the singers actually understand what was involved in learning the music at hand? I wanted to diagnose their ability to work in groups at a shared musical task. Second, how good was I at setting up new and different experiences for the choir's growth and enjoyment? I wanted to test my own skill at changing the "Do what I tell you" rehearsal format (which I enjoy, but which needs variation) to keep the choir's interest and my own.

Doodling with a pad and pencil, I wrote a list of what is usually necessary to a "standard" choir rehearsal. Here are typical activities required of singers in an effective rehearsal:

Listening to directions
Following directions
Learning correct notes
Singing pieces without mistakes
Practicing clear diction
Producing clean attacks and accurate releases
Observing dynamic markings
Being familiar with the correct ("my") tempi and interpretations

There is nothing wrong with those requirements. Any director would want such things to be happening in a well-organized two hour session.

I turned to look at the director's activities. What would I be doing to bring this list into being?

Accomplishing my musical objectives
Achieving a musical result
Feeling (being) in control of the choir
Playing accompaniments well
Keeping the rehearsal well-paced with variety, humor, insight, and brilliant teaching
Inspiring the choir to its best effort

Once again, the list looked acceptable and proper. But both lists reflected problems. First, I had written a scenario in which I was the star of the show. How could people in the choir take a share of the task if I was telling them what to do all the time? The singers were supposed to "listen" and "learn" and "produce." I was taking all the responsibility ("control") and I had better be "brilliant." (Unfortunately for my ego, I had written the lists honestly to see exactly how they came to mind without checking myself for modesty or diplomatic phrasing. Try it some time.) The result of my lists: too much work for me, not enough responsibility for them.

What's more, the activities on the lists didn't look very *interesting*. Music teachers are always telling us that practice isn't always fun, that everyone gets bored, that you must keep at it, that life's like that. But I couldn't accept these homely truths in this situation.

I work with volunteers. If they aren't having an interesting rewarding experience in the choir, why should they take the trouble to come to rehearsal at all? I had to offer something genuinely involving, something that would engage interest and encourage growth.

The lists seemed to describe too much "practice" and not enough "learning." I wanted to replace a "do it over and over 'til we've got it right" experience with a "discover, share, experiment, and succeed" experience.

I'm engaged when I'm learning. I'm bored when I practice. Isn't this true of most of us? Besides, life can be boring enough without dull church choir rehearsals. Even if directors are interesting sometimes, or even often, I had to admit that even I wasn't all that interesting all the time.

But what activities would show that learning was taking place? What did I want to see? I made a new set of lists. My first list shows the activities taking place in a learning experience for the choir. I wanted singers to begin:

> Helping each other
> Identifying problem areas
> Saying "I have trouble" with particular spots
> Asking for help—from me
>       from each other
> Learning to learn a new piece—
>       questioning
>       examining
>       reviewing
>       analyzing
> Learning actively rather than accepting directions passively
> Making mistakes without fear or worry (to avoid that awful timidity which haunts choral attacks)
> Thinking "We will perform well because we can learn," in-

stead of "He has to teach us because we don't learn very well"

Gaining confidence as individuals and as a group.

And what about the director? What would I be doing to promote this flurry of active learning? I would be:

Explaining the evening's activities

Limiting tasks to those most likely to succeed

Deciding what skills were important for singers' development

Recording events for study later to evaluate the rehearsal for me and for them

Gathering singers' feedback

Identifying strong and weak points in the rehearsal format as it took place

Dealing with singers' resistance to an unfamiliar rehearsal experience, if necessary

## The Plan

To make all these activities happen, what design would do the job? How would we actually spend our time doing things to learn, grow, and get involved?

Planning a two-hour experience, I sketched:

| | |
|---|---|
| Analyzing music in small groups | 30 minutes |
| Sharing results, working on problems | 30 minutes |
| Break | 10 minutes |
| Run-through of music rehearsed | 40 minutes |
| Evaluation of the rehearsal experience | 10 minutes |

The choir had worked in sectional rehearsals before, so it seemed safe to assume that they could work in sectional groups. But how would they know how to analyze a score? They would need directions.

Rather than give verbal directions, I would provide each group with a handout. It would be a group responsibility to read and share the ground rules rather than my role to dictate and enforce them. Direction handouts would be the same for all small groups.

Cruising about from one group to the next, I would compare

the behaviors of each group, take notes and be available to answer questions, or give clarification if needed. Singers would share the task, and I would simply watch to make sure they were making progress.

### Directions
"Working as a group, please list below those spots in the music which need particular attention tonight.

Identify as much as you can for concentration, e. g. intervals, rhythms, words, breathing, dynamics.

Try to identify what needs work without running through every note of every piece. The only object of this task is to see what needs work. We will work on actual learning later in the rehearsal.

Make sure that each member of the group has included what he/she wishes to work on.

Please call on me if your group would like help."

Now that the plan was complete, the advantages of the evening looked guaranteed. Groups would be contributing problems on their own instead of my specifying them. We would really be working together on a shared task—actively examining the music and coming to grips with its challenges. After the break, a run-through of all music would show both the singers and me how much we had accomplished.

The second hour would be a real reward for the work of the first hour. Notes would fall into place. Singers would be confident at meeting the music, examining, and then beginning to master it. We would all look forward to the next rehearsal when those extra touches of polish and musicianship could be applied to the upcoming performance.

Oh, it was a lovely dream. What's more, it seemed to make sense, and although I wasn't sure what would happen, such good intentions could only lead to success. A mysterious feeling of uncertainty only seemed to make the prospect more exciting.

To make sure that there would be some written record of the choir's delight with my brilliant plan, I devised a questionnaire. To be answered in the last ten minutes, it would show people's reactions to the evening, help evaluate my design, and see how singers were progressing as musicians. If there were any problems in the rehearsal, the questionnaire would reveal them. Also, by answering my cunningly devised questions, the group would be growing in the process of making music, not just taking another set of orders from the Big Chief.

## Questionnaire

Which part of the evening was most helpful?
Least helpful?
Most enjoyable?
Least?
Did this session provide any experiences you might not have expected? What were they?
Should we use this format: (please circle one)
Always　　More often　　Regularly　　Sometimes　　Never
Could you list quickly any advantages or disadvantages you see in the way we worked tonight?

　　　　　　　　　Advantages　　　　　　Disadvantages


Could you list any specific or general things you feel you learned this evening?
Was the purpose of this evening's session clear?
Did we use the time efficiently?
What do you hope we can accomplish at the next rehearsal?
Are there things we should have done tonight we didn't do?
Please write any other comments or suggestions.

And so, what happened?

## Small Group

The tenors and basses working together might have been rehearsed for it. They shared the directions, appointed a recorder for the points they would make, and set to work. They pinpointed spots where breathing might be difficult, identified tricky rhythms, questioned pronunciations in the church Latin, and concluded their task after almost half an hour to the minute.

They were relaxed. They laughed. They worked easily together. The experience looked ideal.

For the ladies, life was different.

"We know all this," said the spokesperson for the altos. I was
not prepared for them to gain *that* much confidence so fast. I
questioned. Well, they responded, they needed a complete run-
through. They wanted the very experience I wanted to avoid.
They had to hear the organ part, they said. They wanted me to
play, they said. They needed to hear the other parts in order to
study theirs, came the voice of the altos.

It was not a reaction I could respond to positively.

By questioning, probing, even being skeptical, I pointed out
that there were tasks they could do in analyzing the music at hand
as the directions asked. My questioning was not easy. I was working with good readers, and they did know a lot.

After some prodding, they agreed to work with the one singer
bold enough to question whether she herself could in fact sing all
the music flawlessly.

One alto, a teacher, chided me: "I know what you're trying to
get us to do. We're supposed to think. It's just what I keep trying
to get kids to do. I may not feel like doing it, but I know what I
ought to be doing."

Although the tone was friendly, the implication that I was
treating the choir the way one treats children came through clearly. Was I? I smiled wanly, relieved that they had only twenty
minutes left.

Little did I know what awaited in the soprano section. First, a
quick profile: Like many choirs in small churches, ours is rich in
sopranos. There are six. They range in age from the middle teens
to the middle seventies. Some read not a note of music. Some
perform in a demanding choral society. The range, then, in age
and capability is the widest in the choir. This disparity, I quickly
learned, maketh not a smoothly running group. They floundered.

"What are we supposed to be doing?" echoed through the room.
And answers came there none. Confusion reigned.

From my training in working with various small groups, I knew
that one should not necessarily intervene in such moments to

"save the group from itself." Often it can be more helpful to a group not to put out a fire, but to see what the fire can teach the group. The sopranos were ablaze.

"I don't know," "I don't understand any of it," "I don't read music, you know."

I waited to see how the ladies would resolve their plight. And I waited because, oddly enough, no one, despite what I had encouraged in the directions, was asking me for help. They were waiting for me to give help. I was waiting for them to ask.

At length, one person went to the piano, asked where people wanted to start, and began to impose order on the chaos.

It wasn't easy.

"Where's Barbara?" asked someone. Barbara had not attended a rehearsal in a year and a half. Yet a spirited discussion arose to determine where she was. Anything to avoid the task in the directions.

I tiptoed from the room to check on other sections.

When I returned ten minutes later, the group had disbanded.

"We couldn't do it," I heard. Another group had formed at the pay phone to call Barbara. "Isn't it time to stop?" asked one singer hopefully.

It was time to intervene. I herded them back to the piano. No one was very excited about returning.

"We need a director," they said.

"I'm not going to say anything," came another voice as I sat with them in a brief moment of painful reflective silence. And then we heard the problems come out of hiding. We heard the fears in public which had been carried around in private for longer than I wished to think.

Readers were worried about non-readers. Non-readers were worried plenty. Each of the non-readers thought she was the *only* non-reader. Those who weren't sure of how much they really did know feared the worst. They pooled the fears. I just listened. They were beginning to uncover reasons long hidden for hesitant attacks in performance and for ambivalent attitudes toward choir singing generally.

Catharsis is seldom easy. This session was not easy.

"I had no idea that people don't know the *simplest things*," cried one singer later.

Finally, pulling itself out of its melancholy, the group agreed to try once more to list the places in the music where they might have trouble. I encouraged, reassured, negotiated, sweated.

In the end, they worked on half the music, and consumed forty-five minutes. I could not let the tension build without hearing it out. I could not let the catharsis occur without allowing another activity to relieve the drama of the situation. They could not fail utterly to complete the task.

And they did not.

Not utterly.

## Large Group

Mercifully, the session with the entire group was better. Taking the sheets handed me by each section, I reviewed with everyone the spots they had identified as troublesome.

Attention was high. Nods of understanding and interest accompanied the work. And, to my delight, the actual sound was more . . . intelligent. I did not hear the mindless, absent quality a small church choir can sometimes make—the not-quite-human fuzzy drone of the uninvolved. The choir *sounded* attentive, tuned in.

Attacks were cleaner than usual. Many dynamic markings were being observed without my calling special attention to them. Best of all, many more questions were coming from the floor:

"Can we do page 3 again?"

"I don't get that lead."

As a reward for the challenge of the small groups everyone seemed more sensitive to what was being learned.

We worked hard, quickly, with intensity.

By this time, the questionnaire would be a risk. It would point up problems as well as the smoother part of the experience. Usually we aim in rehearsals toward that final few moments where we sing our best piece, or loudest piece, or softest piece—something that will let us all leave feeling good.

I gambled, feeling it was more important to have the questionnaire's feedback than to have a minor glow. Singers pondered and wrote with ominous quiet. The thoughtful looks and intense writing told me that good commentary was in the making. Somehow, as people finished, they seemed reluctant to leave the room. They could almost be waiting for more singing. They rose slowly, lingered to talk. It was a good sign that people could resist the urge for speedy escape, at any rate.

## What They Thought

No one found the first activities of the evening particularly helpful or enjoyable. At least no one was admitting it. Despite what I had hoped for—and what I had seen with the men—the data showed little enthusiasm for self-directed learning in small groups. The choir was voting for work in a large group with me at the helm. Not very original, not very innovative, but undeniably the will of the group.

Then the surprises began. First, only one singer out of thirteen said that we should never have a rehearsal like this. Eight said we should use the format sometimes, and two supported its use regularly.

If nobody was supporting the small groups as helpful or enjoyable, how could so many be willing to do it again? Either I had mis-designed the questionnaire, or some other factor was at work. Maybe they wanted to tell me that they would go along with changes if I wanted (such are the patience and charity of many church groups). Maybe they didn't want to hurt my feelings. Did they know what contradictory data they were yielding?

Was the moral, "Whether something is fun or helpful doesn't make a difference if the leader says it's good for us"?

Only seven responses arose from the question about learning. Maybe they didn't see rehearsals as learning, or I wasn't making rehearsals learning experiences or both. Finally, only seven (the same ones?) had suggestions about what might have happened in place of what we had done.

One disturbing interpretation of the data came floating to mind. Perhaps only half the choir could comfortably comment on the rehearsal experience. The others, less verbal, or less accustomed to being asked for their ideas, did not seem in a position to contribute very specifically.

Watching behavior at rehearsal, I could see that people less aware of rehearsal procedure were less active. The more they knew of what was aimed for, what was going well and what wasn't, the more they could involve themselves in the activities of the evening.

Those who wrote most, commented specifically, and made the "best" insightful musical comments were those with the greatest awareness, the greater musical skills. The writers were the leaders, the helpers, the pro-active musicians. The quiet ones in the questionnaire were the quiet ones in rehearsal.

If this supported the thesis that you're a better choir the more you can contribute to the direction of rehearsals, it also showed much work remained to be done. Not only would a large group in the choir need help with learning about music, they would need practice in looking at how they were progressing. They needed to know more about how they learned.

The challenge was becoming: "How can we make a learning group out of a performing group?" How could we respond to the "I come to sing, I don't come to learn" members of the group?

Performing ability without learning ability just can't exist. Yet our singers often feel that performing is their skill, their contribution. To challenge that skill and ask them to submit to training is a sensitive undertaking.

In a daily life where so much is difficult and demanding, singers come to us to sing, relax, feel good about an activity they want to believe they do well . . . naturally. Can we tell them that music, too, makes demands without discouraging or seeming to reject them? The questionnaire was yielding more questions than answers.

But it was yielding some rewards as well. Advantages in the evening included: "Teamwork" (someone had seen what I hoped for), "Discussion helped identify problems" (that's right, that's right) and "Speaking out."

Disadvantages included: "Not enough singing time on each piece," "lack of leadership" (how could I promote a discussion between this commentator and the "Teamwork" writer?), "Jumping from one piece to another too rapidly."

Not only were the comments evaluating our rehearsal, but they were also providing important guidelines for any future rehearsals with this group. The choir, as teachers enjoy saying, was teaching me. It was showing me how to give direction so that members' views and individual styles could be accomodated.

But the group was teaching itself as well. They were learning: "how others felt about the music (the other altos and their needs)," "how to count each rest and what the dots were," "my weak points," and the intriguing statement that "scores can be accomplished with ease as long as there is enjoyment."

That last comment came from the jolly men's group. Could the lack of response have come from the hapless sopranos?

"If you liked the rehearsal you learned something." Was that the conclusion?

What did people find during the evening which they might not have expected? "Help from unexpected quarters." "Having to think!" "I learned to speak up, also not to depend on memory so much." "The discussion of parts at the beginning brought out mutual problems." (Was this a beginning to see that problems could be shared instead of held fearfully inside?) "I learned that others have more trouble with reading music and counting than I thought."

Here were the learnings I had hoped for in the first lists. Not many, maybe, not exactly as I had phrased them, but here they were: the vital human aspects of learning, awareness, questioning, discussion, and helping. The choir was beginning to discover what I wanted them to experience and use.

What's more, the opportunity to write general comments yielded astute insights to guide future planning. Singers noted:

"A feeling of being needed is important."

"Perhaps I did not get full benefit from the session, but I can see reasons for doing it the way you did."

"This might work better with fewer pieces of music."

"I just like the actual singing together."

"I feel strong need to take home music and work with the piano to nail down tricky intervals."

"Next time have everyone sing the songs, go over them at least twice, and then find out what bad points are."

Finally came the prize essay of the entire exercise. One soprano, Susan, was so involved with the experience that she could barely be persuaded to give me what she had written. Her reluctance raised the question of how singers can tell the director directly how they really feel. How easy is it for "rank and file" chorus members to treat their leader as an equal human being? A frank and helpful relationship always takes work, and choir relationships are no exception.

With coaxing, Susan agreed to let me have her comment.

Did she let me have it!

"I felt the first part was generally not useful in that we only vaguely understood what to do—and did not want to do it that way. I personally could have gotten a lot out of it if the others had not had so much trouble, and I felt it was unfair to place them in such a situation.

"I feel that the self-help idea has much to recommend it if the people are on the same musical level. Maybe it *could* work, but we were unable to make it do so.

"An encounter group should be composed of people who *want* to join it.

"You seem to have an idea of how things should work, but it seems to me to be very theoretical and iffy. Perhaps you should *consider* the possibility of giving it up."

She might not be enthusiastic, but she sure was involved! To create and sustain dialogue of such candor and clarity would be a major step for any group, and a unique one for a choir.

Months later Susan and I were still discussing choir problems. The "encounter group" aspect of the experience, a risk, had produced the involvement it was designed for. Much as I was concerned about the note *(it* got *me* more involved than I expected), it seems a landmark of progress in the choir's self-awareness and, eventually, self-direction.

## Said and Done

What did this experience mean for the choir? How do we assess the changes we feel are necessary in choirs and their activities?

This two-hour rehearsal produced an enormous amount of paper data—more than twenty pages of lists, notes, plans, and questionnaires.

Although not every new experience produces a like amount of material, it may produce important insights for action. A musician or committee concerned to evaluate the workings of a program could easily collect such materials for study and discussion. The exercise might make a significant difference in the operations of a church's music. It might even motivate people to consider further changes, improvements, or further study.

Probably the self-study induced by this rehearsal was the most important contribution to our music at this time. Some insights were planned to occur, others occurred by accident. And yet the accidents were almost "planned" so that behavior of both director and singers could be reviewed and examined.

## Review

How was this catalytic experience set up?

*First,* a list of desired activities was drawn up by the director. From a study of the list came implications, such as the hope for new behaviors, through helping and analysis in groups, to replace the old behaviors of direction and repetition.

In setting goals of new behavior, it was important to include what the director wanted as well as what the choir needed. Although there might not be direct influence from the director to the choir, there needed to be a viable role for him. It was also important to see the experience as a way to keep the director stimulated and involved with choir work.

Without the ability to stimulate and involve himself, how could he do the same for others? The threat of being bored—even mildly—with musical activities can be fatal, not only to the musician's career, but also to the activities of a volunteer choir. The presence of novelty, challenge, and even experimentation can be the spice of a church's musical life.

*Second,* the rehearsal design aimed to enhance people's effectiveness as learners as much as their effectiveness as performers. A new balance between learning and performing was set as a goal of the evening. Choir and director were expected to learn by using new behaviors, taking notes, and developing sensitivity to both music and people.

*Third,* the activities for the evening were custom-made to fit the aims after asking questions like:

What activities are appropriate?
How much time will each activity take?
Who will be involved and with whom?
What materials or resources are needed?

Often activities and objectives in a rehearsal may not "fit" easily. The "how" of what we're doing may not suit the "why." I tend to use activities I know because I know them, enjoy them, or do them well. Similarly, the choir enjoys singing music it knows. The trouble, then, is that my pet activities may not give the choir what it really needs, and the piece they "know" may not yield a very exciting or even musical performance.

Neither objectives alone nor activities for their own sake would have been as effective in guiding this experience. It took both a list of hoped-for results and a new set of activities to shape the two hours logically.

It was not by accident, then, that the alto said, "I see why you did what you did." Without such a visible logic in the plan, the choir could have had a larger dose of confusion than it experienced even with the carefully devised design we used. Without the plan, singers would have been hampered by more uncertainty and ambiguity than they could handle.

*Fourth,* data was recorded both during and immediately after the rehearsal. Director's notes included descriptions of behavior, direct quotations from singers, and times when particular events took place. Notes after rehearsal included my feelings, hopes, concerns, and sense of what was right as well as what was wrong with the session.

A tape recorder preserved the doings of the large group, with the group's permission, and provided material for later rehearsals when we listened to particular problem spots used as illustrations in the choir's progress.

With tapes and notes and questionnaires, all of us were involved in examining the rehearsal. From our findings came important points for planning based on specific comments and reactions.

## Summary

To sum up what happened—good, bad, or just noteworthy— I made the following lists of observations:

- The design of goals and activities was well executed.
- Another time, I'd share the design with people in the choir (a steering group), ask for input, and modify accordingly. Singers have fine instincts about rehearsals and could be used more in planning. Few wished to discuss planning after the fact. They needed to feel consulted first.
- Questionnaire responses were thoughtful and helpful.
- Next time I'd share the written directions in a large group before setting up small groups. The small groups felt isolated and uncertain about the total plan for the evening. "Contracting" with the whole group—explaining, clarifying, asking for their assent, changing any needed parts of the plan—would have won support, or at least approval, for the new design. I failed to do this because I feared "losing" ten minutes at the beginning of rehearsal. The resulting confusion took more than extra time and effort to correct with damage to soprano morale as well.
- The experience yielded enormous learning for me.
- Next time there might be a verbal evaluation by the choir recorded on tape rather than on a questionnaire. This sharing allows the group to review activities together and feel that they have been heard. The social aspect of the rehearsal would also be enhanced by talking as colleagues rather than by writing down "answers for the teacher." The questions answered in writing could easily have been discussed in a round table format.
- I still did most of the planning and learning.
- An ongoing group which meets occasionally to discuss the group's development could be an enormous asset in making the creative experience of planning, change, and learning into a richer shared undertaking.

- Almost everyone had a new experience.
- Next time, there should be some definite next steps articulated before people leave. Where is all this leading? What did we do this for? What happens now? So what? All these questions may be in the air consciously, or unconsciously. A concluding statement about the use of the rehearsal, the reasons for it, and the follow-up to it would be helpful.

As it was, the evening didn't appear to feed in logically to a plan for the preparation of Christmas music—our stated purpose in meeting—or did it seem to contribute clearly to the overall development of the choir—my cardinal concern.

Singers can easily assent to a plan which makes sense if they share a sense of the plan. In this case they were too reticent or polite to ask what in heaven's name I was up to. Some guessed, others approved because they liked me, and others just held back disapproval or simply let it go.

Not every rehearsal takes twenty pages of planning and analysis to describe. Not every rehearsal needs to be an adventure into the uncharted waters of innovation. The follow-up rehearsals to this experience were more "traditional" in response to some singers' reactions.

But this rehearsal kept on having an effect. More questions were being asked about the music; more analytical behavior, more comments, and more concern arose. Suggestions were more frequent about possibilities for the structure of future rehearsals. People began to discuss the development of skills and repertoire to help the choir keep growing. A course in music reading was organized. What's more, the performances for the month between this rehearsal and Christmas were among the best the choir has ever produced.

Using the performance record as evidence, it seems that stopping to look at what you're doing, making experimental plans, and analyzing operations do not harm the making of music. Fear of "losing time" in the process of revising methods or practicing new behavior in rehearsals was unfounded in this case. Creating awareness of rehearsal behavior and individual needs may be even more important than performances we created. Change, learning, awareness can begin to be crucial ingredients in the choir's involvement and musicianship.

# 7

## MUSIC AND MANAGEMENT

More than colleagues in other branches of music, the church musician is a manager. He plans programs, motivates singers, assigns tasks, directs projects, and takes responsibility for a large portion of the church's program.

For musical roles (teacher, performer) we can find formal training. But for the role of manager we are seldom trained at all.

Since most musicians are an intelligent segment of the population, they learn quickly that needed management will bring results.

Peter Drucker, in his book *The Effective Executive* (New York: Harper and Row), claims that effectiveness—the ability to achieve results and not just work—is a skill which can be learned. He identifies five areas of activity which help managers to be more effective. Exploring these areas, musicians or committees may develop new management skills for better music.

The Five Activities of the Effective Executive

Activity 1: Using Time

Let's watch a busy music director at work minute by minute. He has arrived at church in the evening since he works elsewhere during the day.

6:45—Rushing dinners like that isn't healthy. Must cut down

on food or take more time. Oh, for time to digest. Hour and a quarter 'til rehearsal. Got to set up chairs first.

6:48—Time to think. Got to put away last week's anthem, set out music in folders. Note: Nancy couldn't find the one with her name on it, and held up starting while she looked. Got to make sure everybody has all music at the beginning to save the scrambling around and confusion during rehearsal.

6:51—Too many chairs. Don't want them looking at empty seats all night. Depressing. And distracting. Bill has a cold, won't be here. Mary away to see her mother. Subtract two chairs.

6:55—Maybe we should sing the new piece first. It's too tough to end with. Could take a long time to get started. Wish Bill were here to see it. He'll have trouble with it later. Maybe we should wait for it 'til he's back. No, sopranos will need all the time they can get. Good grief. Six sopranos and two altos, how can I get some of those girls into the alto section? Wish we had more readers.

6:59—Folders out, old anthems stacked to go back to library, new ones on top. How did last year's Easter leaflet get into Jim's folder?

7:02—Time out to look at accompaniment for the new piece. Wow! I'd forgotten this is no cinch for me. Look at those triplets. How does he play this on that record? Oh yes, oboe on the swell and then a big chord, fast manual switch, change of key, change of time. Maybe if I practice now and play it for them they'll get a better picture of the piece.

7:28—Some day I could be a really good organist. Time to try this on the organ.

7:37—Oboe's perfect in that tough spot! There are rewards to this job. Think I'll look at Sunday's organ stuff while I'm doing this well at the keyboard. Oops, it's back in the music library. Oh well, I have to look up the postlude anyway. Why do I leave the practicing 'til Thursday just because Sunday went well? Why can't I get more time to practice?

7:41—Organ music ready to go. "Hi, Barbara. You *are* early. How're the kids?"

7:50—Hate to break off conversation like that but I had to

finish the practice on the new piece. "Well, hi Jenny. Glad you like it. It's the oboe stop. Sounds just like an oboe, that's right." Why do I use half my practice time talking? Can't they see I'm working?

7:55—I give up. Besides it *is* time to rehearse. Are those chairs right? Ohmigosh, the folders. No time to look at the music either.

7:59—Well, about half here, but we better start—the only way to show we mean business about starting on time. How will they use time well if I don't?

Look familiar? What's actually been accomplished?

Threat of indigestion and accumulated fatigue haunts our friend's activity. "If tired and in doubt about what to do, keep moving," he seems to feel. Set up chairs, shuffle music, try something on the piano, ponder the current choir problems (each week has new ones), get to the organ, greet the singers, discover the time's gone.

But was the rehearsal planned? Is the new piece now in hand? Will it be played for the singers? What decisions were made about the evening? What did actually consume the time? Let's see:

Chairs—seven minutes
Folders—six minutes
Piano practice—twenty-five minutes
Round-trip (organ-choir room) twice—six minutes
Finding music—three minutes
Small talk—six minutes
Organ practice—eight minutes (five the first time, three the second)
Thinking and puttering—fourteen minutes (in pauses of one or two minutes)
Total: seventy-five minutes or an hour and a quarter.

How do we feel after an hour and a quarter in this situation? Do we have a feeling of accomplishment? Is the work under control? How well will this rehearsal go? Notice that no concentrated activity took even ten minutes except the piano practice, the activity least relevant to the evening's work.

Here's a different kind of time record from another music director:

6:45—Time to relax and plan the evening. Sit down with a pad and paper and see what has to be done until seven o'clock. Then do it.

6:59—O. K. Plan complete. Here it is:

7:00—Review tonight's music for rehearsal at the piano. Note problems for me at the keyboard and for them. Determine order of music. Jot ways to get the results I want.

7:15—Go to organ with Sunday's choral music only. Make sure it's ready for rehearsal.

7:45—Return to choir room, set up chairs and folders, greet singers, be prepared to start on time. Maybe have early singers help with the housekeeping.

8:00—Start rehearsal.


The second director seems to have things together. First, he claims fifteen minutes for himself to relax and plan. Instinct tells him that a frantic pace will not help his dinner, his disposition, or his work. That rushed feeling will rub off on singers too. He's going to stay loose and plan deliberately before he actually *does* anything.

Second, he has a full fifteen minutes at the piano to focus on the coming rehearsal. Some practice is involved, but keyboard work relates to choir needs.

Third, a full thirty minutes at the organ will answer his need to work on his own music. Planning ahead, he'll save the round trip and search for music which hindered the first director. The time is arranged to be uninterrupted.

Housekeeping chores, which won't demand the concentration of other activities, are last. Chairs, folders, and small talk may be combined in the pre-rehearsal segment. Singers may be involved to help. Most important, vital planning and practice activities have been accomplished.

Hectic lives can force us to use the improvised one-piece-at-a-time-as-fast-as-you-can method of the first director. We could come closer to the pattern of the second to be more effective. Hard work alone doesn't guarantee we'll be effective, but planning our time may make the difference.

Try keeping a time log of activities. See if music and your peace of mind improve. It's a way to arrange longer periods of focused activity instead of short periods spent catching up or trying to "cope."

## Activity 2: Making a Personal Contribution

The effective organist has particular strengths.

"You should hear our guy play Bach (improvise interludes, interpret hymns, get that old music box to sound like Westminster Abbey)."

Everyone has a pet specialty. Why not maximize it?

Many responsibilities often mean we're spread too thin over all of them. The risk is that we may maintain mediocrity, winding up like a friend who once claimed proudly to be "the world's most adequate harpsichordist."

Even among highly skilled musicians, few are universally gifted. Brilliant recitalists may play very ordinary hymns. Practicing our hymns—careful gradations of registration for different verses, interpretations of text in phrasing, judicious tempi—may win plaudits for hymn playing, even if we aren't impressing our audience with our modest postludes.

Effective performers need effective skills. They do not need to be sophisticated ones, but they need to be recognizable. We can play accompaniments well and be proud of it. By knowing our own specialties we can make special contributions.

A music committee can identify special contributions the music program makes. Reviewing the musical life of the parish, it can determine the need for strong hymn singing, and the importance of strong hymn playing. Or, recognizing the special gift of an organist who makes modern music come alive, it can build on that skill to give the parish program a distinctive slant.

Trying to do everything because we think we ought to is no fun. Like the director with his time and his nerves in fragments, a musician who wants to make everything a masterpiece without regard to his special skills is wide open to failure.

We may need to be generalists, but we need not be hacks.

Self-acceptance which identifies personal strengths as well as weaknesses is a vital musical tool. Even if our natural gifts seem modest to us, they can be priceless additions to congregations who look to a musician for something special.

Try making a list to answer the question: What can I contribute?

The effective musician makes an effect because he is working with particular skills rather than generalized good intentions.

### Activity 3: Exploiting Strengths

What are the strengths in our church situation?

How do we make them productive? One device for determining strengths is an inventory of strengths and concerns. For example:

| *Concerns* | *Strengths* |
|---|---|
| We have no altos | We have a good soprano |
| Our men can't read music | They come to every rehearsal |
| The organ has a colorless ensemble | But it has beautiful strings |
| The congregation mumbles | They sing old favorites lustily |

Often new strengths appear during the course of a program (new singers join the choir, a violinist moves to town). Strategies to use strengths and address concerns can bring major improvements.

A strength to some may be a problem to others. An organ vapid and outdated to the organist may be mellow and sweet to the congregation. The minister's wife may have a repertory of inspiring song gems from her days as a voice student, which hardly inspire the director. Clearly, strengths are most useful when determined and shared by a committee or when they can yield audibly successful results.

Usually strengths in a church music situation are not directly analogous to strengths in a symphony orchestra or professional group. But shared particular strength goes further than generalized patchwork.

If a choir lacks tenors, baritones can sing a unison line in a piece for them or in a larger work. The minister's wife may be encouraged to share some of the insights of her voice lessons with choir members. She can share a skill she enjoys and raise awareness of what is involved in practicing that skill.

To make musical groups look good, we build on what they're good at rather than covering up what they aren't, or leading them into ambitious efforts impressive in some settings—but not in theirs.

When we hear, "My, that anthem was difficult this morning, wasn't it?" was the choir successful? Or is it scoring points for good intentions?

Once strengths are identified and utilized, they have an uncanny way of leading into new strengths and skills, building confidence in further ventures and new growth.

## Activity 4: Setting Priorities

How can priorities or limitations be set in a music program? If people want anthems, handbells, junior choirs, pageants, organ recitals, and folk songs, what comes first?

First, someone has to say no. Usually it is the director. A committee can be of invaluable help here. Not that everyone on a committee will agree on musical priorities. But a committee can air sides of the priorities question, and face the fact that church music cannot do everything.

What priorities will make it to the top of the list? Drucker says that most of us spend our precious time sustaining the efforts of yesterday. Our orders of service, our rehearsal formats, and our music itself derive from precedents set in the past. The task of "bailing out the past" is not easy.

Yet nothing new is easy either. Often we must decide between yesterday and tomorrow. Where will our energies be directed? Drucker favors a decision for tomorrow. He says that leaders have a duty to plan for tomorrow—before the rest of the organization does. If musicians are not involved in future planning, who will be? Who will make the future of church music if not us? And where if not in the churches?

In setting priorities, the future is a first priority. And how do we act on it? A radical prescription says: drop anything we do which, if we had a choice, we would not start today. "Traditional" snatches of incidental music, the weekly anthem, whatever isn't rewarding to us can go. Cutting back yesterday's projects is the primary way to free up energy for projects to make tomorrow better.

It's no small order. And it takes courage. Courage—not analysis—can be the key to setting priorities. Courage to work in a committee which must decide what comes first, courage in facing clergy who expect that music can accomplish five or six simultaneous objectives.

Courage is indispensable to effective musicians.

We know that we cannot learn an organ piece by practicing a few scales, running through a piece, trying registrations at the same time. We must do one thing at a time, so that the sequence of our successfully completed tasks will yield a polished and artistic result.

The same "one thing at a time" rule applies to our total music program. A small church can always excel at one thing, even if it is simple, such as singing the Doxology supremely well. If we can determine what single activities—focused and diligently pursued—will be our business, we can be more effective.

Drucker gives four common-sense guides for setting priorities:

> Pick the future as against the past;
> Focus on opportunity rather than on problem;
> Choose your own direction—rather than climb on the bandwagon; and
> Aim high, aim for something that will make a difference rather than for something that is "safe" and easy to do.

The last rule may not be quite right for parish church music. Aiming for success can pay off, even if it's easy. After the first success, it makes sense to aim higher. After an initial failure the next step into the future is much more difficult.

### Activity 5: Making Decisions

Musicians make decisions every day. At the keyboard, in the choice of choir repertoire, and in the planning of musical programs we decide the most effective use of our abilities and resources.

How do we make our decisions? Five questions can help musical decision-making.

1. Is this a generic root cause problem or an exception?

In designing the modular music program (Chapter 5) for instance, the church addressed a root cause problem: people attend choir rehearsals in varying numbers at varying times.

A decision to maintain the old program would have meant continuing to cope with this recurring set of changes. Instead, we adapted operations to the underlying realities of behavior.

Many of us treat absent singers as "exceptions" to a once-valid assumption that "every singer attends every rehearsal." Because in reality every singer did not attend every rehearsal, we decided to change a program which was forcing the choir and its director to keep adapting to "exceptions." Finding the root cause problem in a situation is the first crucial step in an effective decision.

2. What must this decision accomplish?

Many of us are pressured into making decisions in order to cope. For decisions to be more than coping—for them to give us direction and problem-solving capacity—they must have particular goals.

"Let's have a children's choir to teach young people hymns and how to read music and work with a choral group" is clearly a more compelling statement than "Let's have a children's choir." Even enthusiasm and optimism can fail if our activities lack goals we can articulate and pursue.

3. What is right?

Every decision may meet with compromise. But compromise is derived from definite positions. A decision made to be popular, or to find acceptance with the music committee, or approximate what we'd really like, is only a half-decision.

Effective musicians can provide a specific vision of what, as executives, we feel is right. After all, we are paid because we know our field and what factors make it successful. We can articulate clear points of a desirable plan to show that our decision—in programming or recruiting or even performance—is appropriate.

We can always use creative compromise. The materials for compromise need to be of the highest quality we can make.

4. What are the commitments to action?

A decision which doesn't create action is not a decision. Where much of the action belongs to volunteers, directors need to know if people will volunteer to support and carry out a decision in the music program. If the music committee decides to introduce a new hymn each month, then someone must select it, post it, perhaps write a note about it for the parish bulletin. Without follow-up in action, a decision can become a non-decision, and the events it advocates are non-events. Tasks assigned and carried out demonstrate that a decision is in operation. A decision without the work to implement it is inert.

5. What feedback will test this decision?

"New occasions teach new duties, time makes ancient good uncouth," says the hymn. Hardly any decision can be valid indefinitely. To be effective, a decision needs periodic validation or change or even reversal. When changes in music are decided, someone needs to check on how well the decision is holding up. Chapter 11 shows a design for one way to collect feedback. Other ways can be devised. Feedback, the contact with reality, will test an effective decision.


Most of us begin to make decisions with our opinions. After all, opinions, based on experience, commitment, and insight, are vital components in our personality. Opinions are important to offer the church.

After we have aired opinions, heard dissenting views, and begun to build alternatives for action, we can check ourselves with questions like Drucker's and select the best final decision.

Thinking and weighing and soul-searching, however, cannot take place with every little decision we must make. The trick is to select and make a few crucial decisions which we will treat carefully. If those few decisions treat underlying realities, they can have the capacity to be effective.

# PART THREE: Relationships

What can destroy the best laid plans of mice and men? Human frustration and misunderstanding—to name two pitfalls in making church music.

If people can support each other and communicate with each other, they can work together. It's easier said than done. But support, communication, and sometimes just caring are human needs in music as they are in any other effort.

Here are stories about people who need each other. Each chapter draws conclusions about how people can be more helpful in the job of music-making.

Working together means concern for individual needs as well as concern for music. Neglecting one concern or the other may spell failure; combining the two concerns can spell success.

# 8

## HOW LYDIA LEFT AND WHAT WE LEARNED

"I just wanted to tell you I'm quitting the choir."

The sentence has many versions. One version tells you she's fed up. Another version tells you she doesn't feel her voice is good enough. Another tells you you're not the one to blame, heaven knows.

Whatever they tell you, it never feels good. We're conditioned to rejoice when we hear, "I'd like to join." We lament when we hear, "I'd like to leave."

The first reaction to "I'd like to leave," is "Oh no." We respond negatively. We feel negative. Instead of accepting or questioning, we simply resist the information with "Oh no." Let's look at a case history.

Lydia had been in the choir for fifteen years. A conscientious widow, she attended rehearsals and services faithfully. She inevitably sent word when she couldn't be present. She enjoyed music, listened to opera broadcasts, and was smiling and consistently cordial.

Parenthetically, after five years I had never heard her voice. Nevertheless, her dependability and ready willingness made her an important personality in the choir.

"I just wanted to tell you I'm quitting the choir," she informed me modestly the week before Easter. "My voice is getting scratchy. I've enjoyed it, but I'm going to leave after Easter."

"Oh no," I said.

She delivered her message in that hectic time after a service, when, I suspect, she knew quite well that a sustained discussion was impossible. She wanted to tell me of her decision simply. She did not wish to be harangued. I suggested taking some time off, hoping she might be persuaded to make her retirement temporary. She smiled and thanked me, and walked diplomatically away.

How and why was this separation occurring? What implications did it have for other situations of departure?

As I pondered Lydia's defection I began to see what had brought it to pass. The insight did not feel very good, but insight is learning. Lydia was making me learn.

First, the choir had been challenged with a new rehearsal format. For her, its lessons about change and efficiency were threatening. Lydia likes routine, and feels comfortable with it. An orderly person, she actually responds better to change than some more open-minded personalities who may fluster easily despite their seeming openness. Rather than quarrel with a rehearsal, she considered its demands and found them reasonable. She simply chose not to fulfill them. She responded to challenge by leaving quietly with a smile and a gracious "thank you."

Second, Lydia had found little opportunity in her quiet way to affect the course of the choir. By her commitment and seniority she could have had a say in how change was taking place. But stronger voices were heard, and Lydia's was not among them.

Did Lydia weigh factors outside the choir? Were there personal reasons for her surprising decision? Too late I was asking, "Why did Lydia quit?" instead of "How is Lydia's life?" when the church might have helped.

The church musician is not officially the person to practice pastoral counselling. But in the future of a musical church, the musician may be able to use a keener pastoral sense than his predecessors. Working with a minister, the musician may need to seek help for a member of the musical group. Pastoral help is not simply to insure that a singer remains functional in the church's musical machinery; it can provide support for someone in need, even in a small way.

What expectations confronted Lydia's choir as a group? Aside from pressures to change, or personal pressures, what pressures operated in the choir?

A church choir is frequently expected to perform well every week, year round, even though musical professionals know that this expectation is unrealistic. No professional group tries for such a marathon record. How can volunteer amateurs sustain it? Many singers feel that they are failing if they do not live up to the expectations. It can be a real problem to provide them with the freedom, rest, or change they need. Musical leadership—director or committee—must recognize this need before others do.

We are not well-practiced in allowing people freedom from the programs we devise. We assume that our efforts will command devotion. Sometimes we have picnics or suppers for "recreation," but essentially we are bidding for time and effort. In Lydia's case we were getting devotion without deserving it. We failed to take the trouble to recognize her need and give this quiet singer a break.

One danger of suggesting time off is that people will misinterpret the opportunity: "We don't really need you that much, so why not relax and not show up for a while?" If the intent of the suggestion is benign, the interpretation can be devastating.

How can we say "We need you," on one hand, and "We can get along without you," on the other? Is it right to call "But we need you" to a departing singer?

The problem is how to express the need. One way to begin expressing needs is to determine our needs more effectively.

In fact the choir did not need another soprano musically at the time Lydia left. She could sense the truth of this, and she acted upon it. What Lydia did not feel was the need for her support and her presence. The choir had been ambitious to produce Easter music, insensitive to Lydia's musical need.

A committee can have a major role in articulating needs, asking for help from appropriate members. No one had asked for Lydia's help for a long time. Instead of being a semi-participant soprano, Lydia might have been invited to full participation in an area where her gifts could make a difference.

Music programs need sensitivity to the deployment of talent. They need to keep people happily involved in projects which make a difference. Lydia's instinct probably told her that she made no difference—a crushing conclusion.

Ecclesiastical mythology to the contrary, no choir needs everybody at every single moment in most programs. A church does have specific needs which specific people may answer. A special service, or a special social event may include those whose constant weekly participation would be neither possible nor, frankly, necessary.

Refining what it asks for, a church program can discard the demand of "needing everybody for everything," a demand which makes the church repellent to some volunteers and just silly to others. Volunteers gladly respond to requests for their unique abilities. They are less interested in jumping on a bandwagon which isn't going anywhere for them.

A volunteer group needs a careful balance: between concern for its job and concern for its people. This balance is crucial to non-volunteer groups as well. Figure III shows a grid representing the relation of both concerns. A position in the top right hand corner of the diagram exemplifies the optimal organization. Most of us have known organizations where one concern—usually production—outweighed the other.

In Lydia's case, concern for producing Easter music exceeded concern for her morale. We needed to address musical goals, and one goal can temporarily eclipse the other. Yet if the work was efficient for Easter it was inefficient later, losing us a dependable member.

Using the grid, a director or committee may make periodic checks on a group and the Lydias in it. A demanding work session may be tempered with a social break. Christmas pressure to achieve special results may be relieved with a Christmas party. Concern for people—their comfort, their egos—can help music as much as concern for musical skills.

When a group helps balance the two concerns (rather than waiting for the director to perform the juggling act alone) the music prospers all the more. Although Lydia informed the director of her departure, she was actually announcing a departure from the group. The group had not made her feel cared for, as much as it had cared for its music.

# FIGURE III

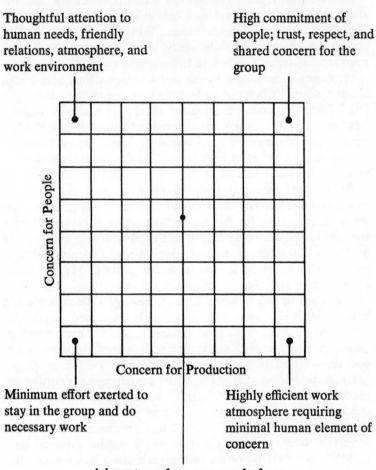

Thoughtful attention to human needs, friendly relations, atmosphere, and work environment

High commitment of people; trust, respect, and shared concern for the group

Concern for People

Concern for Production

Minimum effort exerted to stay in the group and do necessary work

Highly efficient work atmosphere requiring minimal human element of concern

Adequate performance results from satisfactory morale needed for producing expected work

A managerial grid adapted from Robert B. Blake and Jane S. Mouton, "Managerial Facades," *Advanced Management Journal,* July 1966, p. 31.

Reflecting on Lydia's departure, I resolved to share it with the group. It was not right that with her record of service she should fade from the scene unrecognized. What's more, in this tiny church, she would not fade easily. People might bemoan her going, speculate, quiz, pester, or fret distractingly about her exit.

Why should there be a stigma in leaving one enterprise for an alternative one? Choirs often feel "joining is good and leaving is bad." Often desperate "hanging on" to singers with pleas, promises, or pressure is unattractive, even offensive. A graceful departure can be achieved from volunteer work. Occasionally the church, if it's concerned with human dignity, needs to help volunteers leave with integrity.

At the next rehearsal Lydia received a short tribute and a round of applause. She blushed and beamed at the attention and praise. The chance for furtive, apologetic, or negative behavior was averted. By drawing on Lydia's good will in the future, we have a good chance of involving her. We all feel better than if we had tried to ignore the event, or felt guilty or blaming about her perfectly rational course of action.

Could we have prevented Lydia's leaving? I think we could have. Using what she taught us, we might have made things different. We could have watched, listened, asked for her comments. Quiet, dependable people may teach us lessons the more vocal ones never articulate.

Lydia assures us that she'll be in church and supporting us. Perhaps in time she'll be interested in singing again. But to prevent one departure, even had we done it with Lydia, is not to solve other problems. Thinking through Lydia's action may help to see some vital problems more clearly. Lydia is not an untypical singer. She is not a crank, or a troublemaker, or an incompetent. She was one of us who chose not to be. She gave us a serious set of questions to ask ourselves when she left.

Given the conditions of the choir, Lydia acted rationally and charitably. She did not storm, she did not blame. She did not dissemble. She had the good sense to analyze a situation we were not analyzing. She had the courage to act upon her findings. She had more understanding and change-adaptive capacity than I was using.

I fretted, I tried to prevent, I was insensitive. I took offense, at least privately.

Lydia may have done us good that she could not foresee. Without panic or blame, choir departures are normal, ofttimes healthy signs. We believe that Lydia left a good choir of good people. Whatever their reasons, departures may be useful for the development of the choral enterprise.

# 9

## BAD TO WORSE AND BACK AGAIN:
## A CASE HISTORY IN CLERGY-ORGANIST RELATIONS

October 15

Dear Jim,

I want you to know what a joy it is for me to be coming to Happydale Church as your new minister. I'm particularly pleased to know that we will be working together, since the Selection Committee told me several times about your fine work with the music.

As you may know, I had considerable music experience at Seminary. Therefore I know how vital it is for God's people to be united in a strong tradition of musical excellence. There will be several changes in the service which I will be making, and I trust we will have the opportunity for even stronger participation.

I look forward to meeting you next week.

Faithfully yours,
George

November 15

Dear Mary,

Well, the new guy is here, and since you asked for a blow-by-blow account, here goes.

The good points first. He sure is enthusiastic. Smiles constantly, wants to please, and full of plans for the future. So much for the good.

All the future is already in his head. He presented me with a booklet of communion service music he wants ready in two weeks (a month before Christmas!). He will pick the hymns.

He's on some worship board, so he's going to use the parish to play out his pet ideas. I wouldn't say this place is exactly "liturgical," but that seems to be the word he's using so here goes.

Sorry to sound so cynical, but what a dull letter otherwise, right?

Merry Christmas!

Love,<br>Jim

November 15

Dear Jane,

I met the organist today at my new church so I'll fill you in, however briefly, on this quick Christmas card.

In a word, I miss you already. How I wish this church observed the tradition of automatic resignations when the new minister appears. But I suppose I'd have to keep him anyway.

The people are impressed, and the choir sounds all right, but he has no sense of worship. If anything, he seems to be against music. I showed him your wonderful book that we used so successfully, and he barely acknowledged it. If there's anything that burns me, it's some prima donna who won't try anything new. This place has got to have some new life after old Stuffington was here thirty years. Music is the obvious place to start, but this guy has the roadblocks up already.

Have a good Christmas. We'll miss you.

As ever,<br>George

January 5

Dear Mary,

Happy New Year, I guess! I'm sorry to be such a sour puss already in the new year, but your Christmas card was so sympathetic, I just had to sound off to somebody, and you're the top candidate.

His Eminence swept into choir rehearsal less than a week before Christmas with an entire musical Christmas Pageant. The church was not so lucky as to have a whole week's notice. He announced it to them in a special letter three days before it happened. I should be grateful for the five days warning I got!

The choir's special music was swept in between the angels and the magi's lines. The rest of it consisted of (get this) a plainsong hymn, a Negro spiritual with flute obligato ("Oh yes, and can you get a guitar to play the chords?"—a quote from Guess Who), and an organ improvisation ("Just play something around 'We Three Kings' while the children leave the chancel"—there was a procession around the church; seems he loves processions) which turned out to last three minutes.

You can imagine how impressed the choir is. And who do they complain to? And who has to pretend like it's all just fine? I may be stuffy, but I do not air my feelings about the clergy to the choir.

Sorry you have to take all this griping. I've suggested that I get together with him once a month, so maybe I can teach him something.

Yours in pain,
Jim

June 1

Dear Jane,

It will be wonderful to see you again for the 4th of July picnic. We're planning our whole vacation around it.

And do I need a vacation! The organist alone could fill a whole chronicle of disasters for my first year here.

Every blessed month I try to make a dent in his armor, and every time I come away with both hands bloodied from the attempt. He tells me what the choir won't like. He tells me what the parish is and what it isn't.

I decided in April that if he wouldn't do anything musically, at least I might get him into some pastoral work. He won't send out "We Missed You Last Week" cards the way you did. He's got some notion about all that shared responsibility stuff they use in those crackpot sensitivity groups, and says he's there to be a musician and other things have to be dealt with in a group, etc., etc.

I finally have just inserted things in the leaflet, and make sure he has them in time to rehearse the choir for Sunday. Even I have only so much time to waste in endless discussions.

Please tell me what to do when we see you next month.

All best wishes,
George

October 25

Dear Mary,

Sorry we only saw you briefly on Labor Day, but you were so good to express a willingness to keep on listening. I'll take you at your word. Get this.

I've lost three altos (we had four, remember?) over the Columbus Day sermon by Guess Who. Seems he thought a patriotic holiday was the time to talk about the election, and the Christian responsibility to vote for those issues which any moral man must . . . etc., etc., and named candidates.

What next?

Thanks for the lovely picnic.

Love,
Jim

October 20

Dear Jane,

This year is going to be different. I've gotten one of the ladies in the Sunday School to start a youth choir. They'll sing something every month in church, and You Know Who can like it or leave. I simply got it started without a word on the subject to him. We've dropped those awful meetings, so that's one step in the right direction. With any luck, the new choir will do the music for this year's Pageant. We hardly had a chance to do anything with it last year, having to include a choir concert in the middle of things! But it'll be different this year. I'll never forget those Pageants we did together.

The woman here was in a glee club in college, and although she hasn't had leadership training, she's willing to try, and it will be a fine experience for her and the children, I know.

Best wishes,
George

December 1

Dear Mary,

It hardly seems like a mere twelve months since the new regime began. Twelve years maybe.

But enough. It's Christmas. Besides, I couldn't help but chuckle over last week. The Reverend appeared with a plea for some special music for the Pageant. Seems the lady he appointed to start a Youth Choir (I was not consulted) has resigned in frustration, and the wonderful project he announced to the parish (and, by surprise, to me) has bombed out. They'll sing "Hark the Herald Angels" with the Choir, and troop on in bed sheets. Madame the Minister's wife is in charge. Ghastly music this year with morale low, but we've had a moral victory anyway.

What a life! Happy New Year!

Love,
Jim

January 12

Dear Jane,

Thank you for the beautiful card with the picture of your Pageant. It made me cry to think of what happened to us here. You wrote that you'd heard from poor Elsie about it, so you can see what we have to cope with.

Jane, I need your advice desperately. Not only has the Maestro ruined the children's choir, by drowning them out at the organ, he's now decided to disband the adult choir. He has these schemes about demanding that they sign up for rehearsals like kids for a baseball team. He says he'll only plan music after a minimum number sign up.

This is tantamount to destruction of any music at all. I simply cannot see how to save the situation without firing him, and I can't see how I can openly dismiss him just now when the people who support him are still likely to be upset after my patriotic sermon. (The intelligent ones here are backing me all the way, by the way, and the soreheads have left. High time.)

Please tell me what you recommend.

Help!

Love,
George

March 17

Dear Mary,

Since it's Lent—season of penitence and temptation in the wilderness—I guess I might have expected the latest. Mr. Minister held a crisis staff meeting—he's talking a lot about crises these days—and accused me of disbanding the choir. He had invited the Christian Ed. Director to help him confront me with this heinous misdeed.

He was scared stiff no one would sign up for choir. The opportunity to leave, like the Columbus Day altos, was looming large before several singers, as I think he sensed.

But I'm learning to be ready for him. I could report I had twelve people committed to working on Easter music, which may be some of our best ever. When I announced it he seemed almost disappointed.

Nevertheless, he countered by announcing a sunrise service with special music (what it's to be I shudder to think) at which a choir will be necessary.

Much as it would delight me to resign, I think it would delight him more, so I'm staying. Maybe I'm just masochistic enough to wonder what he'll try next.

Happy Easter!!

Love,
Jim

May 1

Dear Jane,

Thank you so much for your words of comfort.

The Easter service was better this year, despite the music which I could barely control.

I am taking your suggestion. We need a committee to enforce some rules of professional conduct in the matter of the organist. I obviously cannot fight this battle alone.

You are much too modest in saying that our dear old music committee is the secret of your success. They hardly met. But you're right that they were supportive in the budget matters. This committee is going to pound some sense into the music program, or I'll know the reason why.

Next year is going to be different.

Your letter has helped make the Easter season even brighter.

Love,<br>
George

December 20

Dear Mary,

Merry Christmas again! How wonderful to get your card and see what great things you've done with the cottage! Everything seems new around here. The choir seems back on the track (isn't it funny how they run in cycles?) and I've had an extraordinary experience with Gorgeous George.

He came to me with a proposal (threat) for a Music Committee. I expressed agreement and delight and said that would be wonderful and a great help to the program and the parish and to me. That was in September. He hasn't mentioned it since.

I think the trick is to agree to his suggestions in principle, which turns him against them. Peace reigns.

I'm even getting used to the Pageant, and although the choir doesn't like the new stuff, they just move through it and do their best. They are a wonderful bunch.

Happy New Year!

Love,<br>
Jim

January 23

Dear Jane,

What a year. Everything's been a mad rush since Christmas,

but since you ask about the committee I blush to say we have not yet had our first meeting.

My organist is a crafty manipulator, and started telling people we would have a committee, and giving people the impression that the committee would be supporting *him*. Obviously I couldn't start anything that way, so I've had to delay.

Now, though, I've gotten some people together to come to a meeting about introducing new music in the church. Our first order of business will be to define Mr. Music's role in THE NEW MUSIC WE WILL HAVE! As you can see, you are my continuing inspiration, and it will take more than a petty reactionary like this to hold up progress around here.

As a matter of fact, Jane, it's highly possible that this will be my friend's last year here with us.

You've always known how much I've admired your work. If the occasion should arise, would you ever consider a move? The town here is charming, and there's a real opportunity. Not that I can promise anything yet. But I am a hopeful man, and feel that perhaps God is moving in a mysterious way in this matter.

We have suffered enough. It's time for a breakthrough.

> With all best wishes,
> George

This little fiction violates the central rule that "every story should have at least one character to like." People are seldom likeable when they are angry, defensive, vengeful, or stubborn.

This is a story without a hero. Both parties act with little regard for sterling qualities which probably are part of their personalities.

Sadly, most relationships in clergy-organist history are this way when conditions of change exist. Polarization, misunderstanding, hidden agendas, anger, and frustration are the materials of this story. Music is only a side issue.

Neither of these people would find much help in lectures about the place of music in worship. Few great insights about music heal wounds arising from threat and counterthreat, thrust and counterthrust.

What, then, is the central issue, the generic problem? Our most frequent response refers to a "personality crash." We shrug away the challenge of a problem seeming hopeless and impossible of action.

What are these people doing wrong? How many actions can you name? Re-read the story and point out how often the organist prejudges, how frequently the minister quite naturally defends himself from the resistance of one who claims he never airs his feelings! Try to identify behaviors which aggravate the situation in each letter. The crescendo of conflict is unmistakable even (often particularly) during the quiet sections.

And this story lasts a long and fatiguing three years! (Many of the true ones last longer.) Yet, the ending—a departure, usually by the musician—is almost inevitable.

When a "crunch" occurs, most of us choose one of three courses of action:[1]

   —Get out (The Maestro yearns to leave).
   —Put it back the way it was (The minister yearns for the
       glorious past).
   —Renegotiate (Neither of them works at this; few of us do).

Obviously, the last and most difficult option is the most feasible for saving a situation such as this.

But how? Challenge the authority structure? "Restructure a decision-making process?" Pious urgings and sunny solutions cannot promise help to Jim and George. These angry people have enough mechanisms in their lives without more machinery.

What does the church say about such problems? Trust, love, understanding, forgiveness.

How do we apply them?

If the situation represented in these letters were one in which a few simple elements could be identified, perhaps a solution would present itself. Persistent problem situations usually defy the accurate identification of their root causes. The factors in ongoing conflict are so entangled with each other that the situation looks hopeless. Nevertheless, one diagnostic format may be of help in a confused set of difficulties.

This format—the Problem Statement[2]—attempts to break

down a situation into component parts. The statement is designed
to answer four essential questions in the situation:

—Who is affected?
—Who is causing it?
—What kind of problem is it?
—What is the goal for improvement?

In a tangled problem situation, answers are not easy.
*Who is affected?*
Jim, George, the choir, the parish, Mary, Jane—all are affected
by the conflict situation. Another way to ask the question, then,
is "Whose problem is it?" Somewhere on the way to a solution
someone must take the responsibility to say "This is my problem,"
or "This is your problem." Someone must say: Who is affected?
*I* am!

Without taking this first step, players in the drama never take
roles in solving their plight. A central figure—one person—needs
to emerge to give some perspective in an ill-focused picture.

A Problem Statement does not thoroughly describe a problem
situation, of course. But it does seek to articulate clearly one
thought-out view of the situation which could lead to improvement. It forces a diagnosis—usually several to choose from. It
leads to a reasoned prescription for action.

The need to be specific is crucial to writing a Problem Statement. Sometimes we feel inaccurate or unfair saying that a problem stems from one person. Yet it is usually true that single people
need help with their problems more than pairs or groups. Providing help for either Jim or George would begin to ease the pain of
the problem, if not solve it. After all, the letters are, in their way,
pleas for help, for support and understanding.

*Who is causing the problem?*
Another way to ask this question: "Who, if approached in this
situation, might be able to change it?" Often problems seem
caused by abstract forces—aggression, misunderstanding, or the
state of the world. Yet it is actual individuals who act out these
forces. It is a single person, likely as not, who can affect the problem in some way.

This question does not seek to fix blame so much as to identify a key figure who may have an active role in affecting the problem situation.

*What kind of a problem is this?*

For example:

> There is a lack of clarity or disagreement about goals.
> There is a lack of clarity or disagreement about the means of achieving goals.
> There is a lack of skills needed for particular activities.
> There is a lack of material resources.
> There is inaccurate communication.
> There is too little or too much communication.
> People have a different understanding of the same thing.
> Roles are lacking or inappropriate.
> Norms are restrictive, unclear, or inappropriate.
> There are conflicts of ideology.
> There is a lack of clarity or a conflict about decision-making, e.g., power struggles.
> Expression of feelings is inappropriate or inadequate.
> There is a conflict related to individual differences.

Several of these may be operating. The challenge of the Problem Statement is to identify the most pressing ones.

*What is the goal for improvement?*

Here is the most crucial question in the Problem Statement. Usually we have so many goals that it is difficult to focus on only one. Ideally, the goal can be described so clearly that there can be no trouble recognizing when it is reached.

One common error in writing Problem Statements is confusing strategies with goals. "Let's have a meeting" is the beginning of strategy for some problems. It's hardly a goal for improving communications problems. A Problem Statement's goal for improvement shows *"what* things will look like" in an improved situation. It does not prescribe *"how* things will be arrived at."

Planning of a strategy begins with the goal provided by the Problem Statement. Attempting to solve a problem before we know what it is seems foolish when we consider it. Yet most of us—unaccustomed to concentrated periods of diagnosis—generate strategies before we have all the information we need. Because problems are painful, we try to make them "go away" quickly. We prefer to dismiss a problem rather than find out what is causing it.

Let's review the case of Jim and George—so rich in possible diagnoses.

*Part I* Who is affected?

Jim

George

Jim and George (This is the least valuable response because, though true, it will be harder to act upon.)

*Part II* Who is causing it?

Jim

George

Jim and George (Yes, but you have to start somewhere.)

*Part III* What kind of problem is it?

Almost every example we saw could be written here. The problem is to decide which category of problem is most likely (or most important) in the situation.

*Part IV* What is the goal for improvement?

The most useful goals are often the most simply stated. Effective goals often relate directly to the remedy of Part III. For instance, if there is a problem of "lack of skills," the goal could be as simple as "acquire needed skills." The strategies to acquire skills and the definition of specific skills could be designed in a later step. The important point in the Problem Statement is to achieve agreement on the nature of the problem. Then the strategies can be generated in a list of alternatives, and the appropriate action selected on the basis of careful diagnosis rather than hurried attempts to "make it stop hurting."

Cases like Jim-and-George are seldom resolved by single prescriptions. The Problem Statement format is one of many ways to approach a painful situation. Those involved in church music need to recognize what forces create problems. If recognition requires games with paper and pencils, lists, T-groups, psychiatric intervention, or binding arbitration, then these are other alternatives to explore.

Strategies are of little use without diagnosis, and without either, the clergy-organist dilemma must continue.

# 10

## PROBLEMS IN HAPPYDALE

A bright opportunity went wrong. Acting out the failures of the ecumenical movement, an experiment in cooperative music failed. And it might have been a success.

As small churches survey their music, they cannot fail to see what choirs, musicians, and the art itself might gain from successful ecumenical cooperation. This little case study is for those who will consider such cooperation. It tries to show, with hindsight, significant problems which, recognized in time, can be solved. It describes a situation which might, in another setting, yield creative and exciting results.

Background:

Within half a mile of each other, in the suburb of Happydale, stand the First Congregational Church (liberal), the First Methodist Church (evangelical), and the Church of the Ascension (Episcopal). Frankly, they don't like each other much. They have tea together sometimes, but basically they are in competition on the same turf. The competition makes them edgy.

Nevertheless, the three churches are very much alike. For one thing, they all deny being alike. In addition, the members are predominantly white middle class Protestants, while the Episcopal rector encourages communion services. Their three foci— liberal, evangelical, liturgical—are exemplary and complementary components in Protestant tradition. Each parish claims between one hundred and three hundred souls. They occupy a small plant and two medium sized plants respectively. Each has a sanctuary, church school facilities, and offices. When this story took place, each church had supported two choirs, senior and junior, for as long as people could remember. Each has a two-manual organ and several pianos of varying quality.

Junior choir enrollments hovered around ten kids per parish, mostly girls. Senior choirs numbered around fifteen adults, predominantly women. All three choirs, perhaps because of proximity to Boston, had been exposed to "above average" leadership and repertoire. Baroque, Romantic, and contemporary composers were represented in the three libraries and sung with varying degrees of success by each group.

The groups had never (as of 1968) sung together.

Although the musicians involved had not worked together, they were a potentially strong team. Two men in their early twenties with intensive musical training were engaged in graduate study (education and theology respectively). A young woman with teaching experience and a master's degree from a respected music school completed the cast. Dan, Stan, and Ann were all respected in their churches.

Beginning:

Dan started things by calling Ann in May of 1968.

"I don't know about you," he said after the preliminary introductions, "but we've only got a handful of kids over here, and I'm not very excited about that small a number next year."

Ann acknowledged a similar situation and a similar lack of enthusiasm.

"How about calling Stan and seeing if we can put the kids together and make a really good kids' choir with our combined resources?"

Ann agreed to this, and Stan, when approached, said it sounded OK to him. The group would meet and rehearse at Dan's church the next September.

Considerable enthusiasm was in evidence at the start. More kids arrived than had been expected. They responded well to the first three rehearsals. Parents were pleased, and clergy approved. Plans were made for Dan's church to host a service of dedication for the new choir, which would combine the three churches in their first joint service.

Dan's church was particularly pleased. Dan had taken initiative, hosted the rehearsals, and taken a leading role in working with the children. He applied considerable administrative skill in organizing the project, and set up the festival service with its following reception. Ann was pleased and offered suggestions.

Stan was less in evidence. He failed to appear at rehearsals for the first month. His school schedule was heavy. His participation was sporadic. Since Dan and Ann had not decided exactly how jobs would be assigned, it was difficult to move without him.

Nevertheless, the service with its large children's choir, its massed adult choir, festival trumpet, and packed church, was a huge success. A new era of cooperation—based on music and children—had begun. The beautiful day, ringing with music, bright with clear fall weather, was a good portent.

Hardly anyone objected to the Episcopal service of baptism which was interjected since the service was taking place in an Episcopal church. How could guest clergy object to the liturgy of their hosts? How could fellow musicians object to the energy and good intentions of Dan's leadership?

What's more, the children seemed to be pointing to a highly promising pattern for the adults. Building on the promise of the first service, the adult choirs pressed for a chance to work together. They produced two subsequent musical services—somewhat less well attended, but still impressive. A spring performance of the Fauré "Requiem"—once again at Dan's church—not only attracted a goodly audience on Good Friday evening, but was presented for a local women's club as an impressive joint musical project. It even attracted other singers from the community who joined to swell the ranks.

In that spring concert Ann played the organ while Dan and Stan conducted the first and second parts of the performance. Stan's participation had been more noticeable now. The united venture seemed to be succeeding in the community even beyond the church settings where it had begun.

The youth choir performed twice more that year, rotating from church to church. This gave the youngsters (as well as the parents) an exposure to varying worship formats. It also meant that each congregation could hear and identify with a group far more impressive than junior choirs of the recent past. For congregations in their mature years, it was heartening to experience youth in good numbers engaged in a worship activity.

In May, Dan accepted a job in a much larger church. He was succeeded by a musician who would also assume youth leadership for the three churches. Encouraged by the choral successes of the year, a joint appointment seemed full of promise to the congregations and Dan felt that the music program would continue to flourish.

How could the promise of such a fine inaugural year be faulted?

Disaster:

Dan's successor was not a success. In the fall he mounted a large, aggressively Episcopal service, with English anthems and liturgical chant. In response, First Congregational produced an austere rite with unaccompanied tunes from the Bay Psalm Book. In the spring, the choirs presented a variety of contemporary music as a quasi-service. The Episcopalian organist, lacking woefully in musical skills, began to lose the support of his parish and, discouraged, failed to produce a viable youth program for any of the parishes. He left within the year.

At Easter, the Episcopal rector resigned, as did the Congregational minister six months later.

Meanwhile Dan was offered a larger salary and was invited to return to Happydale. Returning, he found the promising program in disarray.

"It's been a disaster," Stan remarked mildly.

In its third year, the ecumenical youth choir consisted of fifteen children, mostly girls, under Stan's exclusive direction. They sang twice in church and produced a jazz cantata in the spring. The adults sang Britten's "Rejoice in the Lamb" on the same program, under Dan's direction. Ann was accompanist.

In the fourth year, enrollment was down in all choirs. The

children sang simple folk tunes once in a church setting, and a simpler pop cantata in the spring. The adult concert consisted of secular "selections," one of which failed badly, and a senior bass in his 70's singing opera tunes to a banjo accompaniment. Attendance at this program in Ann's parish hall was less than forty. The Episcopal choir did not participate, although Dan assisted. Promise of refreshments failed to attract a crowd.

Stan resigned that month to join a rock band.

Slow Motion:

Let's look at this experience again in slow motion. What was happening that made this plot proceed the way it did? Were the seeds of disaster inherent in the fruits of the first year? Or did something go wrong later? Was it just one of those things?

Before reading further, try jotting down or discussing the case. Try asking "What should they have done?" or "What shouldn't they have done?"

What Went on Behind the Scenes:

Notice Dan's first statement in launching the project. It has several contradictions. First, he doesn't want a small youth choir. Assumption: youth choirs need a large number. Yet he accepts that a youth choir is worth working on. Why?

The churches never discussed why they were having a youth choir. Choir aims, or results, or character never came up. As it turned out, such a venture did not really appeal to two out of the three musicians. Yet they accepted it as necessary and decided to try it together. Music committees did not question closely. Church school staffs were mute.

In Ann's response, she expresses a similar concern about small numbers. Both musicians agree to collaborate to avoid something rather than to embrace something. They avoid small numbers and head for big ones. They fail to state purpose or check out the assumptions behind their actions.

Stan readily agrees to the scheme and then opts out of its vital planning stage and early launching efforts. Neither colleague settles this with him until much later.

Leadership roles are not defined, nor are tasks assigned. It

seems assumed that ecumenical cooperation, of its intrinsic good-
ness, can sustain the project.

How does it happen that Dan's church is so prominent in the
first year?

As it happened, Dan was the spearhead of the project. Stan
was uncommitted, and Ann stepped aside. Dan failed to recognize
the need to build a team. Therefore, if problems arose, Dan would
solve them before sharing them with his colleagues. Ann did little
to challenge Dan and Stan did not feel impelled to share any feelings of concern. He felt mildly remorseful at his beginning behavior and could hardly say that Dan's work wasn't effective. Dan
came on so strong that neither colleague confronted him with
many modifications.

Furthermore, Dan's rector took similar initiative in service
planning. The germ of resentment about the baptism rite grew. It
confirmed the other clergy in negative impressions of Episcopal
polity, rigidity, liturgical pretense, etc. Dan did not make sufficient
effort to involve both clergy and musicians at the beginning stages.

Speaking of the clergy, what were they doing to help? Precious
little. The joint service which had gone so well almost guaranteed
an anticlimax at the next occasion. Nobody likes to be an anticlimax. If the rector had been over-assertive of his prerogative,
the minister was almost passive. He planned a loosely focused
worship service with little relevance to the rather ambitious music.
Musicians were once again uninvolved in the laissez-faire service
planning. The self-fulfilling prophecy of anticlimax came true at
the subsequent "not-so-well-attended" service.

Was this problem discussed by the leadership? It was not.
Amalgamation more than cooperation seems to have been the
foremost goal in the musicians' minds. Amalgamation—to what
end—was not explored. What's more, no one wished to disrupt a
feeling of amity which seemed to be in the air. To discuss a problem together was too threatening.

But of course problems were discussed. Those who felt the
Congregationalists weren't living up to the glorious Episcopal start
were quick to say so. Those who felt that the Congregationalists
had been co-opted, said so also. In each church the pattern of

distrust was going on as ever, with everyone cautious about bringing up a sensitive issue.

By presenting the Fauré "Requiem" as a concert rather than
a service, the musicians neatly circumvented the clergy. Avoid-
ance did not solve the problem of service planning. Perhaps the
musicians were working together well and the clergy were not.
However, as we have seen, the musicians were none too steady in
their team effort. Neither among the clergy, then, nor among the
musicians, nor in a combined group, was the issue of "How Are
We Working Together?" discussed.

To review thus far, a goal-less enterprise was being implement-
ed by an unformed team. Yet the enterprise, given novelty and
proximity and homogeneity and a big push from Dan, was being
successful.

Actually, Dan was not too happy. He found Stan's vacillation
disappointing, and did not sense real support or help from Ann.
He also felt that the baptism had been a tactical error. He had
concerns to share with a total group. Yet he was so invested in
making the project *(his* project) work, that he failed to share
his concerns with colleagues or clergy in any church. In the end,
he chose to leave Happydale with its problems of collaboration
rather than stay to work with them. (This choice, he soon found,
didn't help him, since similar problems arose in the new church
which could not be addressed because of a rigid internal parish
structure.)

Parish feelings, clergy feelings, musicians' feelings—none had a
real hearing. Yet a creative job description was devised for Dan's
successor in the program's second year. The polite Christian
community would bury its reservations and launch the second
stage to a well-launched project. Who could find fault with such
behavior?

As events proved quickly, the decision to leave a major leadership role in the hands of one person was disastrous. What seemed
like a sensible outgrowth of the first year was actually a continuing abdication of responsibility by Ann, Stan, and the clergy. That
they failed to recognize their abdication made the new man's
failure doubly damaging. Had one person not had such leadership

thrust upon him—a role he wrongly and strongly accepted, to everyone's later regret—things might have been different.

In the second year, leadership did little to improve the lopsided arrangement of responsibilities. The impending departure of clergy might be one reason for this. The musicians by now were being worn down by a poorly designed working relationship. Commitment was waning on every front. At this point, there could have been an analysis of problems. Saying there was a "personality problem" would not help. Several objective, understandable flaws in the program might have been addressed. Non-commitment, politeness, and dismay ruled a situation where candor, concern, and faith might have helped.

Throughout, the choir had had no say in any of the program policy. The choice of difficult contemporary music or denominationally tinged repertoire was not helping their morale. Seldom, if ever, were they asked to help lead the project. The seeds of choral disillusion were being watered by this lack of input. The "disaster" Stan mentions had spread through a goal-less, half-planned program to a now almost destroyed leadership team and an increasingly disgruntled rank and file. These problems were many times more threatening to discuss than earlier ones. Therefore, those involved understandably chose not to evaluate the deeply troubled program. However, they agreed, still believing in the magic of "cooperation," to continue with the help of the returning Dan.

In the third year, joint worship was abandoned, once again evading the clergy. Stan took full responsibility for the youth choir, rendering cooperation impossible. And Ann formalized her subservient role by being accompanist for the spring concert, planned and conducted by Dan. Feminists might point to Ann's acting out the "feminine myth" of docile acceptance in this situation. Ironically, the program looked smoother as it took on a less cooperative quality. Musicians worked separately. Clergy were troubled not at all. Policies were still unformulated, people still unconnected in their lopsided configuration of responsibility.

The results of the regressive third year came quickly in the fourth year. Stan's single-handed work with the youth choir meant lack of support in the other two parishes. Enrollment and program suffered. Dan, now sensing the deep troubles of the program at last, felt unable to confront new clergy or his colleagues. Discouraged at last by the fate of what he had begun, he too opted out of taking responsibility.

He had felt alone again in the spring concert, scheduled at an awkward time. Stan had made a conflicting appointment, cut rehearsals, and almost failed to appear at the performance. With the kids to worry about, he didn't work much to support Dan. Besides, he was contemplating his own exit as the two clergy and Dan had done in the two previous years. Once again, failure to involve the singers in planning weakened participation. The secular program was designed without Dan. (He had scheduled a conflicting appointment and agreed unenthusiastically to abide by what "they" might plan for a change.) Ownership of the enterprise was dead on almost all fronts. The resounding failure of the spring concert might have been predicted.

In four years the project had moved from a promising start to an inglorious end. Instead of a model of cooperation, Happydale had been a pathetic example of mutual self-destruction.

Morals of the Story:

The reader can record his own morals from this sordid little saga. Obvious ones may be set down in the following checklist.

1) Are the clergy equally, actively, and genuinely involved in the project? They wield influence and make decisions which can kill or save the undertaking. Happydale clergy failed to be equal, active, or genuine in their roles.

2) Are musicians likewise involved?

3) Are there clear goals towards which the project is addressed? Togetherness is nice, but it wasn't enough in Happydale.

4) Does the project have a long-range plan? Happydale's music went from point to point in spurts. A reasonable plan would have helped to begin and then to sustain it, clarifying everyone's understandings over time. A plan can always be modified. A lack of plan makes problems and confusion from the start.

5) Is there a base of support in parishes, committees, and choirs which will sustain the project? One way to gain support is to ask for help in planning. It does not pay to wait until dissatisfaction arises.

6) Are tasks clearly assigned to individuals? Sharing is easier if the terms of the partnership are as explicit as possible. Ann's role as accompanist in Happydale's third year made her and her colleagues more comfortable with their work. Ambiguity about responsibility can be wearing. It can be avoided.

7) How is music selected? See Chapter 4 on resources.

8) Are people's feelings being shared with honesty? How can people be kind if they don't know it's called for? Candor is priceless. If in doubt about feelings, try asking simply, "How do we feel about what we're doing?" and be prepared to be honest and diplomatic.

9) Is there a plan to evaluate the project on an ongoing basis? See Chapter 7.

10) Can the project survive an early success and still look closely at the possible problem areas before they become unmanageable?


At its best, the ecumenical challenge can lead to enormous reward. The checklist from Happydale is one step to begin.

# 11

## DIRECTIONS FOR DIRECTORS

Informal singing—just for fun—has its own rewards. Here was a new and helpful experience. Although choir directors wish to be benevolent, even placid, mild-mannered musicians may become autocratic when placed in front of singers. Of course this seldom applies to church musicians. Nevertheless, I discovered that my own behavior was startlingly revealed last summer.

A soprano from the choir invited me to sing madrigals in a quartet. Here was a real fix. Singing madrigals is a praiseworthy activity which any musician, especially a choir director, should endorse. I was not enthusiastic. First of all, I had never sung madrigals in any group. Second, this group was to be tiny and my mistakes and ignorance would show. Lastly, I seldom sing anything except to show the choir what it's doing wrong. "No choirmaster can sing," I quip to myself and the choir, "that's why I direct."

What to do?

Not wishing to be rude, I didn't see how I could refuse. I pushed myself to agree. Would we like to sing some (pleasant, slow, easy) Tudor anthems, I asked. Perhaps I could save face by starting with something I knew. No, said the soprano. The group was interested in (fast, chromatic, in Italian) madrigals. Real madrigals. Trying to sound positive, I agreed to round up some music and bring refreshments.

Armed with new music *(The A Cappella Singer,* ed. Clough-Leighter, E. C. Schirmer), we began the next Thursday.

To start with, there was a good bit of aimless chat. Drawing from my experience with groups, I could almost have described us as "avoiding the task." I took heart. Perhaps we were all a little apprehensive about diving in. I certainly was not about to suggest we start. Here was an unusual stance for a director—always the one to take the lead in herding singers to their battle stations for rehearsal.

At length when we could stall no longer, the books were opened. The alto kept exclaiming with delight over the familiar treasures of our new collection. The rest of us enjoyed her enthusiasm, hardly knowing how to respond. She became our leader, picking the first selection. I remembered times when I have worried over vacant looks at choir when I unveil a challenging new piece. One's own uncertainty is only sometimes reassured by someone else's enthusiasm.

I moved to the piano to pick out notes. It was also my task to sing tenor, a part with which I had no experience at all. Forced to learn something new, I'd figured, why not learn something completely new? This was lucky, since I had been called in the traditional absence of a tenor.

My first lesson was quickly learned: I could not play four parts and sing at the same time. Aspects of the problem cropped up in quick succession:

> My ear is attracted to outer parts, not to the inner ones.
> I need training to listen to one part out of four.
> I can cover up vocal inadequacies by playing the piano.
> Since I could not listen, I could not blend with singers.

Finally came the unkindest insight of all: all these problems were arising from a situation which occurs every week at rehearsals! I was acting like a director to the detriment of the singing and the group.

Sheer habit had sent me to the keyboard and prompted me to feel responsible for everyone's notes. The result: I couldn't sing my own part, and lagged far behind when we sang without the piano. The moral: directors are just as likely to lag behind a group as singers, especially when they're "helping" instead of listening.

Next time we had the alto pick out parts while I muddled along as best I could. Things were much better.

As we gained confidence the baritone suggested trying a second piece.

Instinctively I flipped to the table of contents. "Got to find the next page number, announce it and get started. Don't want to waste time." I stopped myself short. Had I been asked to make a selection? Habit told me it was my responsibility. Reason told me otherwise. After all, we had time to choose together, and besides, I didn't know the music!

I shared this thinking with my friends. We laughed and agreed it wasn't necessary. Control, long an admired skill in conducting, was inappropriate to the occasion. Letting things relax to find a joint selection was more comfortable for me and for the singers.

Applying this insight to the choir, I made time for the choir to select some music for itself. Fifty anthems from the library were set out on a large table—buffet style. As they encountered works they liked, singers wrote titles on paper provided. Although this method did not determine *all* the music we would sing, it identified some music we would *not*. (To my surprise most had tired of familiar titles I had thought they cherished.) Most important, this activity gave a feeling of ownership to those who'd helped make choices. People seem to relate better to tasks they help create, than to tasks they are assigned.

Now it was time for me to start singing in earnest. The predictable came true. I was dreadful.

I seemed to make at least three kinds of sound: head tone falsetto, adolescent-sounding chest tone, and a bleating pseudo-Caruso noise created to avoid the first two. My companions were sympathetic and intrigued as I was with these vocal oddities.

So unlikely were my utterances that they prompted a brief discussion about placing the voice, and keeping quality even, natural, and supported with enough breath throughout the range. We taught each other aptly and to my surprise. My lesson was that usually I give mini-lectures about the choir's mistakes. It never occurs to me to discuss my own.

The discussion yielded two advantages: the sound improved as we listened more closely and became more conscious of vocal techniques. What's more, we had begun to build a team-like feeling of US to replace the more accustomed feeling of ME and THEM. Additionally I was hearing the musical insights of singers who had much to tell me. Finally the exercise had been a set of reminders from ourselves to ourselves; the kind of group feedback I've been trying to foster in rehearsals of the large group.

As I made more mistakes we patiently corrected them. The value of the learning went far beyond the notes.

One result of this mutual help experience is that the choir now uses more small groups for learning. The large group works at coordinating what we've learned. This can have human benefits in feelings of mutual support and help as well as "covering material" more efficiently.

Finally our summer experience—relaxed and informal—made a significant point. Unpressured by demands to perform (most choirs must perform, ready or not), we were free to make mistakes, to take our time, to learn at the pace which seemed best for us. We even selected several pieces—needing much study— simply to play with. We found ourselves building a readiness to perform. As we sounded better (like most musicians we were self-critical and not easily satisfied), we began to think of seeking occasions for performance. This is a new pattern for me who had always thought that a group needs an occasion looming ahead of it to pressure people into working.

It seems that growing comfort and competence can create the desire to *make* occasions for music. Fewer demands for a choir's public performance might help the group make better music as well as an authentic desire to create it. No services go better than those for which the choir is prepared and enthusiastic.

I made a checklist of what I've learned from my madrigal adventure. Here's what emerges:

> Mistakes are good for you even (especially?) if you're the director.
> Learning from friends, peers, is a good feeling.
> Without pressure to perform, motivation need not slacken.

Listening and empathizing can sharpen a director's skills.

Non-direction can be helpful to a group's development, induce learning, and, as Shakespeare says, "Thus by indirection find direction out."

The director takes chances with his assumptions and his self-esteem when he joins a small singing group. Yet the chances are worth taking. Singers can move from large groups to sectional groups to mini-groups comfortably in a supporting and friendly environment. The mini-groups create more musical independence and the ability to listen as well as to build a vitally important spirit of team cooperation.

The chance for mutual help and learning is a rare opportunity. If directors can experience that opportunity, and then provide it for singers, choirs can be more musical and more humane.

# PART FOUR: Futuring

Future challenges to church music may not always be musical challenges. Their solutions may not always be musical solutions.

Musicians may be asked to provide many kinds of resources and skill in tomorrow's church.

Leadership will need to be of high quality to insure a church music for coming generations.

These chapters examine new ways individuals and groups may approach the musical enterprise.

# 12

## THE ACTIVATED CHOIR

Belief in technology threatens churches. Electronic organs replace "real" ones. Rock bands make our choirs seem more and more out of touch with reality.

Is there a way to use new developments as helps? Yes. The methods outlined here are new, but they are practical and possible. If they don't make a choir completely self-directing, they can make it more active, run more responsibly by singers.

These approaches aim to upgrade the director's work rather than to eliminate it. The more a choir can do for itself, the more advantages accrue to its director.

### Individualizing

This fancy and ambiguous term can have many meanings. One way to involve individuals in a group is to give them individual experiences as well as group experiences. A common practice—letting individual members take music home to learn at their own pace—is an example. That's individualizing.

Another example is to tape parts, or have singers tape them on a cassette recorder. The recorder may be carried with (or to) any member who misses a rehearsal. Tapes can be left at church or at a member's house where singers may drop in and learn parts on their own. Some groups leave the tape on a channel in the language lab of a local school or college. Singers can rehearse themselves at their convenience, at their own speed, playing what they need for themselves instead of having a director pound it out. Cassettes are especially handy for singers who work on rehearsal nights or can't attend particular sessions.

## Using Small Groups

Studies in human dynamics indicate that small groups have advantages big groups don't have. People often speak more freely in them, for instance. They can relate and listen to each other better in a small group than in a large one. This fact is heartening if your choir is getting smaller!

How do you capitalize on this insight? First, small groups can use the tape cassette trick to individualize learning notes for their particular group. All the altos can huddle with the recorder until they're confident of their notes. Groups can learn words together until they're memorized. Singers become less dependent on their music, more likely to watch the conductor for leads. Small groups will readily study words, listen, and help each other memorize, enjoying the exercise as well. Knowing words, singers will anticipate the word on which they come in, ready to form the necessary sound before the attack rather than during it. Result: cleaner, firmer sound on first notes. By using tape and small groups to teach words and notes (once the job of a lonely director pushing a patiently suffering group), mechanical aspects of the choir's job can be accomplished without the director!

Obviously, such a new approach requires preparation for the choir. Small group activity might be only a start for part of a rehearsal. Taping might be introduced gradually, first to the large group, then small ones, then with individuals.

Singers may not believe in their own learning capacities at first. They may be timid. The director needs to believe that they can do it before they believe in themselves. With patience and tact and humor they *can* do it.

## Gathering Feedback

Once notes and music are learned, a group is ready to criticize its own work.

To start, the choir sings without any direction, spoken, conducted, or suggested, from the director. Sometimes this experience isn't easy for a sensitive director! But if he lets singers perform on their own and asks, "How did you like it?" he may gather some remarkably accurate comments.

"We dragged at the end," "We're flat on page six," "We better learn our alto lead."

The choir begins to direct itself. The director becomes a helper: setting tempo at the end, giving hints about staying on pitch, reviewing the alto lead.

As he listens to the choir's critique, he can record the comments on a blackboard or large pad. This way singers create their own checklist to guide them as they sing. The choir makes itself aware of particular spots in a piece where sensitivity is needed.

Of course, if the choir thinks everything it does sounds great, you have another problem! If they don't like the sound they say why, and suggest improvements.

### Taping Rehearsals

A strong director can listen to the sound of his own voice and his choir's without wincing. I couldn't. But at some time, perhaps when the director must be absent from a rehearsal, a choir might use tape to rehearse itself by itself.

In a self-directed rehearsal, the choir distributes music and warms up. Then they tape a piece members feel they know well. Playing the tape back, they comment on it, keeping a record of comments posted on a board. If notes need work the choir members turn to cassettes. If words are a problem, small groups may be called for. Using the checklist derived from hearing the tape, they begin to identify problems and work toward solving them. If problems persist when they tape the piece a second time, they note difficulties on the checklist. When the director appears next, they are ready. They know what they need to work on, and what help they need.

The process might begin in short segments of rehearsal time—twenty minutes without the director. Then, as singers become more at ease with listening, commenting, and making lists to improve, the director can leave for longer periods. Eventually, the director could miss an entire rehearsal without interrupting choir progress.

What are the advantages of a choir directed more actively by its members?

*Variety.* Rehearsals can feature many activities simultaneously: some singers studying music alone; others working on words or at the piano in small groups; others practicing parts with a tape recorder; others listening to a full choir tape to report their findings and recommendations to the choir. The director, if an organist, could be practicing Sunday's accompaniments so the choir may hear an accurate reading with the correct registration instead of a hurried makeshift reading. Another group could simply chat or have coffee.

Like an "open classroom" full of informal learning activities, the choir rehearsal can cater to different personal styles of work. It would offer relaxed, humane interaction. The rehearsal "workshop" would help develop individuals' skills while forming a more skillful musical group.

*Sensitivity.* How can we expect singers to become more sensitive musicians if we're always telling them what to do? A more active rehearsal is an opportunity to spot mistakes, discuss interpretation, and listen carefully to progress.

*Team Work.* A group which shares a task draws closer. Each member becomes more responsible to teammates. New members feel they are joining singers sharing an enjoyable activity rather than some task force taking orders from a Maestro. Instead of comments like: *"He* wouldn't want *me* in choir since I don't read music, have a good voice, have what *he* wants"; why not reports like: "We started a new piece at choir and we made more mistakes together! We were awful at first, but we're getting better. . . ."

*Efficiency.* With a varied number of activities available, a singer or small group can work on what is most needed. Singers have an uncanny instinct for knowing what they need. Those who need note-study can work on that. Sections ready to test themselves may do that. Those who'd just like to see a friend before working may socialize.

*Integrity.* A choir achieving skills in active learning could make each meeting a musical experience. Think of rehearsing a sensitive group with words and notes learned, and even insights on interpretation. Churches could attract directing talent by offering superior musical working conditions.

*Satisfaction.* Self-reliance takes time to develop when singers aren't used to it. But the feeling of "We did it ourselves" is a priceless reward in active musical learning in groups. Increased self-esteem can contribute to music and to the whole church enterprise. Risking occasional mistakes is largely offset by success in learning, confidence, and skill.

These advantages are only some aspects of the activated choir. There can be problems (see Chapter 6). Activating choir rehearsals is not so much a set of activities as a realm of activities. Each church may devise its own most appropriate means of evolving active learning experiences.

Here's what happened using one form of activated rehearsal at our church: First of all it was too easy. Nobody complained. Few even questioned the new style of work. The self-directed rehearsal to prepare for Easter went smoothly. The choir even asked to use the format again.

In three rehearsals of two hours each we learned a plainsong chant with handbell obbligato, the "Gloria" of Mozart's Twelfth Mass, a Latin motet, and an ambitious English anthem.

As singers first arrived, they were directed to sectional groups: sopranos, altos, and men. Each group had a list from the director outlining tasks for each group to do in the first forty-five minutes ("Learn Mozart words, sing notes to plainsong, first two verses without the piano . . .").

The director's role was that of travelling advisor to various groups working on their listed tasks. I watched as the sopranos wasted time in chat, but noticed that if I waited they would move back to the task and work more efficiently on their own in their own way than they might have for me.

In small groups leaders emerged. More able singers, instead of waiting in restless boredom for others to catch up, actively began to lead the group toward their level of skill. I learned some new ways to teach as well!

In the second hour of rehearsal singers laughed together as they made mistakes without directions from the accustomed source. Instead of my pointing to their shortcomings, they were finding their own mistakes.

As criticisms were recorded on newsprint sheets, they became reminders for the next run-through. Small groups used brief phrases as pointers for work ("Altos watch pitch on page 4," "Everybody keep the tempo so we don't go flat . . .").

The obvious need for sustaining the tempo was a primary lesson. Later, rehearsing an ecumenical group, the same theme arose when I ceased to conduct: No matter how much the conductor waves his arms, the real pulse which makes rhythm comes from the singers themselves. The performance—with each voice synchronized in a carefully blended ensemble—reinforced this point.

In fact, so often were pitch and tempo linked as vital to each other that an odd side benefit occurred. On Palm Sunday the minister planned an outdoor procession to "All Glory, Laud, and Honor." As the choir left the church in song, I resigned myself to their leaving the pitch as well. To my amazement and theirs, they returned to the building's rear door after an absence of six verses, still in the tempo they had left with, and still singing in the right key. Without the organ!

Choirs may not need all of these new techniques at once. Even one at a time, choirs may find them useful. A completely self-directed choir may be a fantasy. But fantasies may help explore ways to create more happy realities.

# 13

## EXPANDING MUSICIANSHIP: NEW SCHOOLS, NEW ROLES

Like much creative work, music is a lonely profession. Solitude is inevitable for those who spend hours each day with only a keyboard instrument.

Because leadership is a lonely business as well, the director of music works alone. He alone may be responsible for the choir, for performance standards, for the congregation's musical life in church.

What companionship is available for the church musician? The nearest colleague is in a different parish with his own troubles. Separated by geography, denomination, or differences in taste or ability, church musicians have few chances to support each other.

When churches were more prosperous, the problem of isolation was not so acute. Every place had, or aimed to have, resources, to sustain a self-sufficient program with a self-sufficient musician. The more self-sufficient you were, the better—and the better off —you were. For many, this assumption still holds true. Musicians in leadership positions were trained to work in conditions of suc-cessful parish life. They usually did so in a church with a desire to use professional training. Now that a musical church is hard pressed for choir singers, music budget, and members, however, self-sufficiency is severely threatened.

Nobody likes to be threatened.

Psychologically, threat to self-sufficiency is particularly trying to the church musician. An organist is, after all, almost always a solo performer. The choral director stands alone "above" the singers, and we are not used to the chummy camaraderie of ensemble players. Follow a director? We *are* the director. That's what we're paid for.

But churches trying to compensate single persons who can play, direct, plan, and implement may have three choices. They will have to settle for less able talent, raise their budgets, or cut back programs. None of the choices seems desirable.

After the shock is over, the question is not "Shall we cooperate?"; it is "How shall we cooperate?"

## Training Models

First, a quick look at two new models for the training of church musicians. The Institute of Sacred Music at Yale represents a new development. Positioned precariously between the School of Music and the Divinity School, its students may earn a degree either in music or in divinity. It may be part-time study for a part-time profession. Yet rigor and integrity are maintained, even though sacred music is cast as a cater-cousin in the family of graduate disciplines.

The Schola Musicae Liturgicae, based in New York's Cathedral of St. John the Divine, is being designed to utilize New York as the scene of seminal musical activity in America. The Schola will aim to use resources of the city, cathedral, and a diverse student population in a polymorphous curriculum to train creative musicians for service in churches.

Both training models are based on an ecumenical premise. The problem is that they seem to be motivated more by lack of resources than by enthusiasm for new relationships. This motivation seems true in parishes as well. The choir festival is more likely to encourage interfaith cooperation because denominational capacities are slim than because of the vision of a united church!

But what structure will support the new and creatively trained church musician? The isolated individual parish with its back to the wall, its defenses up, and its resources down?

Support Models

Briefly, two kinds of support systems for musicians in churches now exist: denomination and professional. They have crucial flaws.

Denominational boards (commissions) are necessarily committed to backing up denominational policy. Episcopalians push the new Eucharist. Methodists push media. Lutherans push liturgical worship. Roman Catholics push hymn singing. The whole may be more than the sum of its parts, but the cacophony of competing denominational stresses cannot help but sound muddled.

What's more, it's devilishly difficult to keep up with what each board is doing. It's harder still to synthesize all their findings, or to transcend a board committed to implementing its own policy. Boards, too, tend to be impersonal mechanisms, more given to pronouncing than to listening, and always open to the charge of isolation from the constituency. Finally, it's hard to tell whether such boards do, in fact, affect parish musical life.

One professional support system is the American Guild of Organists. The monthly magazine, *Music,* carries articles on organ playing, organ building, music reviews, and Guild news. Most news stories recount the successes of university or metropolitan parishes in producing programs of professional-caliber music. Consisting of some 17,000 musicians, the Guild has an elevated statement of purpose:

> To advance the cause of worthy religious music; to elevate the status of church musicians; and to increase their appreciation of their responsibilities.
>
> To raise the standard of efficiency of organists and choirmasters, by examinations to evaluate the training and the attainments of the candidates in Practical Organ Playing, Choir Training, and the Theory and General Knowledge of Music, and to grant certificates in Service Playing, and in the respective classes of membership (Fellow, Associate or Choir Master) to candidates who pass these examinations.
>
> To provide members with opportunities for meeting for the discussion of professional topics, and to do other such

lawful things as are incidental to the purpose of the Guild.

In practice, the Guild is as successful as its local chapters, which, like choirs, have good and bad years. Seldom does the Guild have direct influence upon churches or clergy. Neither supports the Guild financially. In some chapters, the Guild works directly with parishes as a placement agent.

All three kinds of support systems help musicians cope with the church. They do little to help them change it. The dangerous assumption behind such help is that coping—especially for those with little formal training—is the most suitable activity for church musicians. This parallels a belief in schools that "slower" pupils can only be given "basics" or "vocational training," while the "faster" students may be tracked into more imaginative, pro-active programs of development. Not only does this assumption waste the talents of those who vary from a single standardized evaluation, but it also reinforces the "inferior" skills of those who conform to that measure. It then widens the gap between fast and slow, professional and amateur, weakening team efforts by musicians in churches.

What is the alternative to being isolated and coping? Being together and developing. Learning less of "What to do" and more of "How to plan." More "Look at where you are and where you want to go," less "Try this, try that, for heaven's sake keep on trying."

The following model—a shared directorate for two churches—employs the concept of team ministry used by recent clergy deployment schemes. Two separate musicians work at two separate locations, yet their roles are "distinctive and complementary" rather than similar or competitive. Salaries are determined by role and responsibility rather than status or tradition. (In education, compensations by responsibility at varying levels is called "differentiated staffing"; it implies more creative deployment of talent as well as a means for controlling spiralling salary costs.)

In the design, a modular music plan would operate for two churches instead of one. A new staffing plan would imply program change. Both staffing and program would change in the sharing model. The purpose of change would be to reach goals of quality, variety, and integrity. Obviously, each church will reach these goals in its own way.

Presenting this idea to committees might involve a document like this:

## A DESIGN FOR THE POSITION OF DIRECTOR OF MUSIC FOR TWO PARISHES

This design recommends that two parishes commission a single director of music to serve each. The director's functions, represented in Figure IV, would be focused on planning and performing the best possible music for each parish.

The director would be largely a coordinator of groups within each parish—clergy, musicians, music committees, and congregations. With these groups he would help to formulate musical policy and devise the most appropriate strategies for implementing that policy. Where particular skills might be needed, as in choral singing or musical decision-making, he would be responsible for training groups in those skills. He would be the central figure responsible for music in each parish, assisted by an organist and supported by responsible groups.

The director's new role would mean a new role for others involved in music. Evaluation of the music would be a vital contribution of the entire congregation. In periodic assessments, they would discuss what goals were important for service music, what strengths could be emphasized, what problems needed work (see Chapter 3). A music committee would take on particular strengthening of important musical tasks (selecting material, recruiting talent). As the director contributes specialized skills, the people he works with become more skilled at support strategies.

A schematic diagram illustrating the place of the director in the proposal is submitted as Figure IV.

The director's salary would be paid by two parishes. In one parish he would receive the salary appropriate to an organist/choirmaster. In the other, where he would delegate responsibilities, he would receive a smaller amount as director, Assuming an average of seven hours per week needed to accomplish the job at a rate of $10.00 per hour, the total yearly salary from both parishes would be $3,640.00, with a month's paid vacation. If the

## FIGURE IV
The Position of a Dual Director:

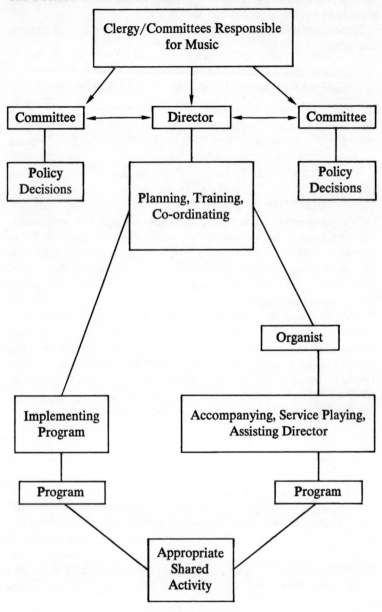

salary appropriated should be smaller, the vacation period might be extended.

The structure represented in Figure IV would have the following goals:

> To develop distinctive and complementary music programs for both parishes.
> To allow optimal sharing of resources.
> To avoid role conflict in shared musical work.
> To encourage the best possible organist for both parishes.
> To use a vacancy in one church in the most creative way for future development.
> To study the proposed structure for a two year period, and report the results for use in other similar parish situations.

The respective committees would be responsible for setting policy to determine how these goals might be reached, or in reviewing them for additions and modifications. (A sample three-month plan of activities is represented in Figure V.) Each parish would authorize the structure and review it in light of the recommendations from the music committee.

## FIGURE V

Sample Activities for a Three-Month Period
Coordinated by the Director:

|  | *Sunday Offertories* |  | *Weekday Activities* |
|---|---|---|---|
| *First Church* | *Second Church* |  |  |
|  | **I** |  |  |
| Choral | Hymn |  |  |
| Choral | Organ |  | Shared music-reading |
| Choral | Instrumental |  | course |
| Choral | Hymn |  |  |
|  | **II** |  |  |
| Solo | Hymn |  | 1st: Choir rehearsals |
| Organ | Choral |  |  |
| Choral | Solo |  | 2nd: Schola rehearsals |
| Instrumental | Congregation sing |  |  |
|  | **III** |  |  |
| Choral | Hymn |  | Shared learning session for |
| Choral | Solo |  | service music. Rehearsals |
| Hymn | Choral |  | for joint services |
| Choral | Guest choir |  |  |

# 14

## THE CHURCH MUSIC COLLABORATIVE

New directions for a musical church can lead to new kinds of
musical thinking. As choirs become more skillful and sensitive
they may wish to take on more ambitious projects. As teams of
clergy and musicians begin to broaden options they may need
new resources. Some churches may find that, as in Happydale,
they have much to gain by sharing. But, as in Happydale, sharing
can make problems as well as opportunities.

How can churches share with each other? How can denominational lines be crossed. How can big churches work with little
churches without threat? How can varying skills, tastes, and
backgrounds be orchestrated into effective partnership?

Many patterns of cooperation are possible. Previous chapters
have shown structures to support single-parish musical development. This chapter shows a different kind of option.

The Church Music Collaborative is a new kind of organization
in its own right. Organizations like it—for sharing resources and
new ideas—already exist in education and industry. But the collaborative model as shown here is new to church music.

The first premise of this model is that every parish is in charge
of its own work. No visiting expert or packaged program can
make success. In a working partnership, each partner has his own
integrity. The Church Music Collaborative aims to strengthen the
identity and integrity of each church involved.

The second premise of the collaborative is that organizations, like people, can develop more fully by interacting with others. Partnership can mean growth for both partners. The crucial factor is commitment: to self and others for development. Yet commitments, like marriage, sometimes lead to friction. Like the honeymoon couple who look at each other in bathrobes over coffee cups after a courtship of champagne and party clothes, the partners may have second thoughts.

But marriage has a two-directional shape:

HE            SHE

while the collaborative has a multi-directional shape and the sharing has numerous facets, as is shown in Figure VI.

How would a multi-directional alliance for the development of each church operate? The collaborative structure as seen in the diagram has a center surrounded by three kinds of member churches.

First come subscribing parishes. By paying a reasonable fee, each subscribing parish would receive a newsletter geared to collaborative goals and opportunities. Clergy, congregations, and musicians would also receive two workshops with collaborative staff on skills relevant to musical development. Each parish would also receive consultation with a staff member. The consultant— using techniques like those in this book—would help groups as well as individuals deal with particular problems and opportunities. Additional consulting help would be available at a reduced fee for subscribing parishes.

Member parishes would receive subscriber benefits with a program of concerts presented by collaborative staff. A member parish would place serious emphasis on a musical ministry. It would work closely with other collaborative parishes and staff in an ongoing relationship.

Leadership parishes would be staffed by musicians of the collaborative staff. They would mount model and experimental programs for development. Resident artists would produce a high level of performance and service and raise a professional budget. Leadership parish facilities would be used for workshops and

# FIGURE VI

## Church Music Collaborative

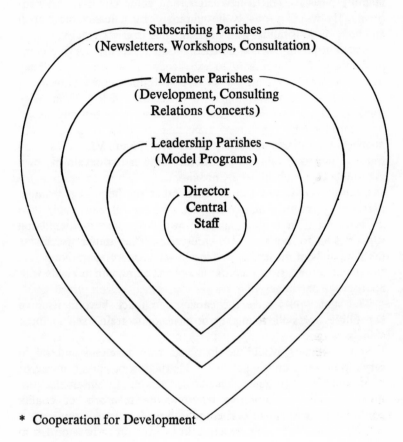

Subscribing Parishes
(Newsletters, Workshops, Consultation)

Member Parishes
(Development, Consulting
Relations Concerts)

Leadership Parishes
(Model Programs)

Director
Central
Staff

* Cooperation for Development

* Sharing Resources

* Ongoing Consultation

* Individual and Organizational Growth

special programs. Apprentices and students would be employed to support leadership staff.

At the heart of collaborative activities would be a director of the staff of artists and consultants. He would help the staff serve member parishes, edit a newsletter, and guide collaborative programs. He would probably be employed by a leadership parish and have responsibilities as a working artist in that capacity.

The central staff would be differentiated and use varying complementary skills necessary to excellence in church music. They would work at leadership parish responsibilities, concerts in member parishes, and would consult in specialized fields. Their work roles would vary as needs differed in the membership and would be determined by functions rather than by title. A central staff member would be more likely to have a specialized professional function in the collaborative structure than he would on his own in a single parish or university or school.

Central staff would call on each other for help as a team in performing, training, and consulting. The central staff would take an active role in evaluating their own work and in identifying support staff for collaborative enterprises. They might also assess the potentials of musicians wishing to serve in collaborative parish situations and assist in the vital job of matching parish needs with appropriate personnel.

The staff would have the capacity to reach beyond its own capabilities for skills it might not have, or to train itself in those skills as needed.

Staff members would be involved with teaching and might serve to accredit colleagues in the instruction of church music or related subjects (organ, piano, voice, choral or ensemble conducting). The collaborative could assure members of quality control in an area where evaluation is difficult to find.

Skills in the following areas would be brought to bear on Leadership parishes and be available to members and subscribers:

Instrumental
Youth music, including folk, pop, and rock
Choral conducting
Liturgy and worship

Organ building and acoustical engineering
Program development, planning, and evaluation
Committee training in process skills
Clergy training in music and leadership
Voice
Music education
Personnel selection
Congregation training

Many of these skills are now available to any parish working hard to find them and pay for them. But they are now coordinated, loosely or not at all, by professional musicians (as in the American Guild of Organists model) without any commitment from parishes. Then, too, model programs now show off the talents of one person, seldom the effects of a team with complementary skills.

The collaborative would seek to make its subscribers aware of the potentials of the music enterprise first. Then, building interest, it would serve members according to individual needs rather than staff interests.

Working together, musicians at the parish level could express needs to be met together (through workshops or specially designed materials like bibliographies or through experiences like jointly sponsored trips or concerts). The resources of the collaborative would be less expensive to a group of churches than to individuals. Individual needs would receive attention through the visit of the consultant and staff offerings.

Unlike supervisors, collaborative consultants would be working toward the goals of each situation rather than imposing a packaged program from an expert or denomination. Unlike "insiders" in a parish, the consultant could bring objectivity as well as skills to jobs like diagnosis and planning in committees.

Each parish in the collaborative would make a musical and financial commitment by joining the group. In return, it would receive collaborative help and support to bring about its greatest potential in music. The collaborative would become self-renewing by continuing to attract parishes at the various levels of membership and by helping each parish to move to the greatest level of commitment and achievement possible.

Money now spent on sustaining the structure of the individual musician, choir, and organist would be re-channeled. It would support efforts of a more skilled staff and more effective use of musical and human resources, both in local situations and in the collaborative as a whole. Resources would be geared toward doing a job rather than sustaining a structure.

As a first step, the collaborative would identify those churches prepared to make a commitment to improve their music. Such churches would also be identifying themselves as open to cooperation and change. They would be more likely to achieve collaborative goals than those who would refuse or ignore membership.

Next, central staff would be attracted by a more professional life of exchange and interaction than they have remaining apart. The graduates of new programs in church music would have a viable organization in which to exercise professional skills. In turn, musicians in collaborative parishes would have the support of their churches in enhancing their professional growth. They would have more resources at their command than if they were alone.

By recruiting membership around shared interest rather than proximity or denomination, the collaborative could avoid the threat to autonomy which collaboration may pose. Often cooperation with a neighbor is more threatening than with someone at a distance. The neighborhood churches of Happydale—in competition—might have used the collaborative to plan, implement, and evaluate their program. A single church might have joined to find resources more appropriate to its needs than those who happened to be around the corner.

Research in the diffusion of educational innovation tells us that new advances usually appear in separate locales rather than evenly in geographic chunks. The collaborative would connect separate areas in a community of musical development and cooperation.

As a launching pad for the collaborative, musicians might use the existing structure of a guild chapter, a grouping of parishes close to each other and committed to collaboration (two or three would probably serve). Stretching a bit, a single parish in search of a focus to its ministry might underwrite expenses of gearing up the collaborative or at least doing a feasibility study. A local arts council or federal grants for arts and humanities might serve as an aiding agency, as might foundations interested in arts development at the grass roots level. After all, a large segment of America claims church attendance, where (whether they like it or not) they encounter music (good or not). A non-creedal project design to develop the capacities of this captive audience and its almost-captive musicians might well earn itself seed money in the early stages.

As support grows among varying classes of membership, the collaborative would seek to become self-supporting through providing services to its members and the community at large.

To a church weary from ecumenical failure and disillusioned by scheme after scheme for self-improvement, the collaborative concept may seem just another air castle of idealism or a clever chimera from the world of theory. Yet, as Curt Lewin says, "Nothing is as practical as a good theory." The collaborative makes no prescriptions or guarantees of particular change or success. It does offer a structure, building on those existing structures in church music, to enhance the work of individual church musicians and to create with their skills a new organizational plan for mutual support and development.

# APPENDIX

## A Format for Self-Assessment[1]

Here are several dimensions of leadership functioning. For each dimension, indicate your position on a scale from 1 to 9. "1" means that your functioning is *totally inadequate* and "9" means that you are *functioning optimally*. Indicate both your perception of your skill and your perception of how an observer would rate your performance.

|  | Your perception of your skill | An observer's rating |
|---|---|---|
| **A. PROBLEM-SOLVING:** |  |  |
| 1. Being the first to see that a problem exists | ( ) | ( ) |
| 2. Identifying the important elements in a problem | ( ) | ( ) |
| 3. Thinking out broad approaches to solution strategies | ( ) | ( ) |
| 4. Working out details for specific action to solve a problem | ( ) | ( ) |
| 5. Selecting appropriate ways to evaluate a solution's effectiveness | ( ) | ( ) |

B. CREATING A
   PRODUCTIVE WORK
   ENVIRONMENT:

1. Motivating others                              (  )          (  )
2. Providing training for others                  (  )          (  )
3. Finding ways to support the
   requests of others                             (  )          (  )
4. Providing direction in
   ambiguous situations                           (  )          (  )
5. Helping others comprehend
   and maintain the focus of
   work                                           (  )          (  )
6. Anticipating how others will
   react to events or actions                     (  )          (  )
7. Orchestrating the efforts of
   groups working on a complex
   task                                           (  )          (  )
8. Allowing others to handle
   certain tasks without
   interference                                   (  )          (  )
9. Giving praise for others' work                 (  )          (  )

C. INTERPERSONAL
   RELATIONS AND
   COMMUNICATIONS:

1. Making your ideas
   comprehensible to others                       (  )          (  )
2. Giving straightforward
   answers to others' questions                   (  )          (  )
3. Bringing knowledge or
   experience to bear in a
   helpful way                                    (  )          (  )
4. Identifying other people's
   main ideas or assumptions                      (  )          (  )
5. Building on the ideas of
   others                                         (  )          (  )
6. Sharing leadership functions
   with others                                    (  )          (  )

7. Acting as a mediator in
   conflict situations    ( )    ( )
8. Handling conflicts between
   you and others with whom
   you work    ( )    ( )

D. WORKING OR COPING
   WITH YOURSELF:

1. Motivating yourself    ( )    ( )
2. Maintaining the focus of work
   for yourself    ( )    ( )
3. Following through on
   commitments    ( )    ( )
4. Managing your work time
   efficiently    ( )    ( )
5. Maintaining a balance
   between personal activity and
   professional activity    ( )    ( )
6. Standing behind what you
   believe is right    ( )    ( )
7. Sharing tasks with others    ( )    ( )
8. Compensating for your
   weaknesses    ( )    ( )
9. Abandoning pet assumptions,
   ideas, projects when evidence
   mounts against them    ( )    ( )
10. Remaining aware of your
    effect on others    ( )    ( )
11. Using what you know about
    yourself and others rather than
    relying on routine patterns of
    behavior    ( )    ( )
12. Following a clearly articulated
    self-growth and development
    plan    ( )    ( )

# NOTES

Chapter 9
1. Adapted from Glidewell and Sherwood, "Planned Renegotiation," in *Current Technologies in Organization Development,* ed. W. W. Burke (Washington, D.C.: National Training Laboratory Learning Resources Corporation, 1972.).
2. Adapted from "Research Utilizing Problem Solving," (Portland, Oregon: Northwest Regional Laboratory, U.S. Office of Education, 1971).

Appendix
1. Adapted by the author from "Leadership Self-Assessment Instrument" (Merrimac, Massachusetts: The Network of Innovative Schools), and used with permission.